Acknowledgements

This book would not have come to life without the encouragement and support of my husband Matthew Ma. It's taken an enormous amount of time to create – time away from contributing to our shared life.

The decision to self-publish also entailed an investment for which the 'return' is simply helping people, most of whom we'll never meet. We made that decision because I didn't want a publisher taking it out of print if it isn't sufficiently profitable. If this book can help one person flourish in life it was worth creating.

I also acknowledge and am deeply grateful to the three dharma teachers who've had the biggest impact on my knowledge and practice. Each has contributed to the quality of this book. They are: Stephen Batchelor, Winton Higgins, and Gregory Kramer.

THE BUDDHA
FOR MODERN MINDS

*A non-religious guide
to the Buddha and his teachings*

Lenorë Lambert

Flourish Press

Sydney

2021

Published by Flourish Press
PO Box 322
Dee Why, NSW, 2099
Australia

Cover and book design by Dani Streay @ An Altered Aspect
Photo by David Cohen

Contents

PREFACE

Is this book for you?

'Can you recommend a secular book for beginners?'
I've been asked this question so many times over the years, but I didn't have one that I could wholeheartedly recommend. There are lots of terrific books but I hesitate to recommend them for beginners because either they assume the reader already has a basic knowledge or they take the religious route, including ideas like rebirth and literal karma, which can be difficult to swallow for Westerners.

The Buddha's teachings are vast and come in many forms, so it took me years to find clarity - to feel I could get my arms around them. I was confused for a long time. As I started teaching, I found that this experience gave me a knack for helping beginners get a grip on the concepts, for crystallising them in an accessible way and helping people see how it all fitted together.

So I decided to capture this in a book in the hope that others might achieve a basic orientation more quickly, especially those who mightn't have access locally to deeply knowledgeable teachers as I've been lucky to.

I've summarised here what I've spent two decades of my life piecing together through a great deal of reading, many podcasts, many retreats, attending dharma groups, and asking all of the 'dumb questions' that occurred to me along the way. (On my very first retreat, Gregory Kramer referred to me as 'the curious one'.)

I originally wrote this book for people like myself: people who are curious to know about the Buddha's teachings but can't accept metaphysical ideas like rebirth if we tried; people who sense there is something real and valuable in there, but who balk at statements like 'life is suffering' and can't quite figure out how this leads to happiness; people who are seeking a less stressful life, or a more rich and fulfilling one.

Many years down the track, I've realised it's also gold for people who've been exploring for a while, and who want a reference book for the basic ideas contained in the teachings. I've sometimes needed to refresh my memory of the many concepts and lists. This book can serve as a quick reference guide for some of those key teachings.

In a nutshell, Siddhattha Gotama was a man who lived in India two and a half thousand years ago. He is commonly called the Buddha which means 'awakened one'. His teachings offer a path to full human flourishing by embracing life - the whole kit and caboodle.

Some pain and unpleasantness in life is inevitable: it's a part of being a human being; it comes with the package. We create another heap of it by our response to unpleasant feelings. Gotama's teachings are a powerful recipe for making peace with the inevitable pain and for letting go of the second dose which we cook up for ourselves.

That might sound interesting to you but there are loads of books on Buddhism, so why read this one in particular?

You'll probably get a lot out of this book if any of the following resound with you:

- You have a curiosity about Gotama's teachings but would like your introduction to be free of the cultural trappings of the Asian Buddhist traditions. Of course I have my own lens through which I digest and present the teachings. The remaining items in this list describe the primary colours of that lens.

- You'd like the teachings explained in a down-to-earth way and in a modern, relevant, non-religious context.

- Your outlook leans more towards the scientific than the metaphysical/pseudoscientific. (Gotama has been called an 'unsurpassed scientist of the real'.)

- Your orientation to choosing what you learn has a practical bent to it. You like to know the 'so what?' of new ideas and you like to road-test them. (Knowing about the teachings won't do much for you. Applying them will.)

- You like to think things through yourself rather than swallow someone else's insights whole.

If that list rings bells for you, then you're likely to find this book helpful.

Introduction

When I started exploring Buddhism, I thought of it as one of the world's great religions. If your starting point is anything like mine, you probably know that the Dalai Lama is a Buddhist and think he seems like a pretty happy chap - not a bad ambassador. You might have heard of Zen but know it mostly as an approach to garden design. You probably think that a Buddha or two adds a touch of serenity to interior decor, perhaps a visual reminder to 'chill'. And you may have wondered why some Buddha statues are fat and some are not.

So it might surprise you to know that Gotama did his best to prevent his teachings being turned into a religion; that the Dalai Lama belongs to a Buddhist tradition that didn't start until 1,200 years after Gotama died; that Zen began 700 years after Gotama died and originally came from China, not Japan; that the word Buddhism didn't exist until about 180 years ago when Westerners claimed to have 'discovered' it in Asia; and that Gotama's teachings could be seen to have more in common with modern philosophy and psychology than they do with religion.

I didn't go looking for Gotama's teachings. I'd set out on my own path of personal growth and I was curious about what it was like to go on a meditation retreat. A friend had sent me a link to one, and I went. That marked the slow and cautious beginning of a turn in my life.

This turn has brought a great deal of insight, a great deal more calmness; less negativity, judgment, anger and stress; more compassion, kindness, patience and love, and a very strong sense of being in touch with reality. It's brought me a way to navigate great difficulties, and to fully experience joys.

The purpose of this book

I've benefitted enormously from the *dharma* (Gotama's teachings and our practice of them). It's as relevant today as it was in the Buddha's time. Its benefits are just as real and the need for it just as obvious.

However many Westerners miss out because the main access we have is through the orthodox Buddhist traditions. These are infused with a world view that is simply indigestible to many from our cultures. I've known people who turned away because they simply couldn't swallow ideas like rebirth, like life being suffering, or karma.

These people have missed out needlessly because these ideas are either misunderstood or not essential to practising the dharma. That's not a speculation, it's an observation from my own life. It breaks my heart that anyone who comes looking for the dharma misses out because of this.

I think many Westerners would 'get' Gotama's teachings and apply them enthusiastically to live more flourishing lives, if only they could find their way easily to the core. The perception of the teachings as a religion can turn many people away from exploring them, either because they already have a faith that they identify with, or because they are agnostic or atheist and couldn't adopt one if they tried.

Neither of these circumstances is an obstacle to becoming a fully-fledged dharma practitioner. The word dharma means lots of things but in this context, it refers to Gotama's teachings and the practice of those teachings. I like to use this term rather than 'Buddhism' because the latter is too easily equated with the orthodox Buddhisms and the religions that have sprung from them.

This preference points to a key purpose of this book: to be a lay person's guide to approaching the Buddha's teachings for the first time in order to see if they might be of benefit; to check them out free of the fear that indoctrination might be lurking nearby or leaps of faith required. You'll find neither here.

Many wonderful books on the dharma are available, books that take a deeper dive than this one, written by people much more knowledgeable of the dharma than I am. This is not intended to be an in-depth investigation of the dharma, but rather a first date with it. It focuses on the big questions that occur to someone wanting to get a sense of the basics, to decide whether they'd like to explore it in more depth.

My hope is that this short circuits a lot of confusion for you and allows you to more quickly and accurately assess whether it's of interest for your life. I hope it will also serve as a home base for the key concepts if you decide to explore further, as even excellent dharma books can often leave people confused if they lack a good grounding in the basics.

My lens

It's important to declare my own paradigm - the lens through which I view the world. Every book has an author and every author has a particular view on things. It's important to know that view so that you can take what I present to you in that context.

I grew up in a family that, despite subscribing to the Catholic faith, encouraged questioning. Indeed it seems I inherited my father's 'built-in crap detector'. Having practised Catholicism for the first 20 years of my life I'm no stranger to ritual and the pleasant feelings that can come with it.

However, even as a young person, my crap detector sensed that ritual was often a mascot given a general's salute. I enjoyed the sense of belonging and community that came with the church, as well as the familiarity and the quiet time with myself in an atmosphere of self-acceptance (which at the time I saw as love and acceptance by God).

But Catholicism left too many unanswered questions for me, too many obligations that I didn't connect with; and told me that as a woman I was relegated to the sidelines. There also seemed to be a big disconnect between the mass and real life, between the way people behaved and spoke in church, and the way they behaved and spoke outside of it. To be a practising Catholic seemed to mean attending mass rather than infusing day-to-day life with the values of kindness, forgiveness and service to others.

As I began adulthood, I was fortunate to benefit from a good education in psychology, a field that, through a strong emphasis on empirical research methodology, instils a strong sense of logic in terms of cause and effect. It's a field that's also concerned with understanding the human experience: it plays in the same ballpark as the dharma. I have an inherent interest in how we humans work, and I learnt a lot from this period in my life.

Fast forward another decade to my mid-thirties when I left a successful corporate career as a director of a publicly listed company. I'd proved to myself and the world that I was capable and had earned more career success and money than I'd ever dreamed I would. While I enjoyed the corporate world in some ways, it just didn't feel fulfilling.

I left for a 'walk in the desert' as it were, a year spent developing a leadership program. This caused me to spend a lot of time on my own, enough time to hear and see myself more clearly. Thus began two further moves in my story that helped form my lens.

The first was the beginning of my own self-development in earnest. I had a lot of baggage I was carrying around. I could see it, I could see many of its effects and I was tired of it. I wanted to let it go. But despite my professional expertise, I didn't know how to do that. So I embarked on my own journey of personal growth involving personal development workshops, some counselling, learning about the dharma and beginning to meditate.

The second movement was that I designed an intensive leadership development program which I ran as my business. This brought together much of what I'd learned to that point, and also stretched and challenged me to grow with my program participants. It was part of my own desire to keep 'sharpening my saw' that led me to attend that first retreat.

This retreat was led by Gregory Kramer, a dharma teacher whom I still see as one of the best examples of beliefs in action that I've ever known. He impressed me not just with his deep knowledge and intelligence, but with his very way of being in the world. I noticed in the moments between sessions that he really seemed to live the stuff he was teaching. My crap detector was calm. That allowed me to explore a bit further .. and to take a turn in the road.

While on the topic of my view of the world, it's probably worth also declaring my relationship to orthodox Buddhism. As Glenn Wallis, an ex-Insight Meditation teacher notes, despite the many and varied approaches to the dharma, an astounding consistency sits at their core. So I feel a sense of kinship with practitioners of these traditions. I also feel an incredible gratitude because, without these Buddhisms, the dharma may not have been passed on long enough for me to encounter it!

Where I part ways with them is if they insist that their own culture's interpretation of the teachings and the practices they've developed are the one right way to do the dharma; if they object to our freedom to do the same thing they did and adapt it to our time and place.

As you'll discover, these traditions sprung up a long time after the Buddha lived and are based on canons created in their own time and culture, not directly on the original recorded version of the teachings. Their translations, interpretations and the out-workings of those are theirs, yet they're often presented as the Buddha's.

Gotama emphasised that the dharma should be taught in a way that was relevant for the audience at hand. He spent his 45 teaching years expressing it this way. Despite this, the teachings have largely been imported to the West with the cultural trappings of the Asian countries from which they came – including some that weren't around in Gotama's day (such as large institutionalised monasteries).

Some people are drawn to this. However, for many others this mode of practice reinforces a sense of Buddhism as a religious in-group that you have to join in order to learn about it. This is not helpful.

The dharma engages intimately with daily life in all its aspects. The rituals, labels, institutions and costumes are entirely superfluous. Practitioners in China, Tibet, Japan, Korea, Thailand and other cultures used them to adapt the dharma from Indian culture to their own folkways and folk beliefs. That was intelligent. We need to follow their process of adaptation to express the dharma in our own cultural terms.

I want to present the dharma in a way that fits both this approach and Gotama's original inspiration - as a way of understanding and living in the world that helps us flourish in life.

So let me assure you of a few things in the hope that unnecessary obstacles don't block your way.

- You won't be asked to believe anything. Gotama emphasised the importance of using your own experience as one of the two key ways to verify what's true. His core teachings are methods for living based on the insights he had through his awakening, not descriptions of truth to be accepted whole or followed slavishly.

- Engaging in rituals is entirely optional. In fact Gotama warned against the over-reliance on rituals as a 'fetter' (a chain or shackle that constrains us).

- You probably won't have to change your lifestyle - the dharma contains no commandments or 'shoulds'. It's about building your own honest awareness of choices and consequences, and then making your decisions in that light.

- A questioning mind is an asset, questioning is good. The dharma works best if you do indeed think for yourself and test ideas fully. There is a saying: 'small doubt, small awakening; great doubt, great awakening'.

Secular dharma

The secular approach to the dharma is an attempt to do what all of our Buddhist ancestors have done: adapt the teachings to our own place and time. The word 'secular' has three primary meanings:

1. Of this age (the root word *saeculum* referring to a lifetime)
2. Not religious
3. The separation of church and state

Accessibility, digestibility and usefulness are the key aims of the secular approach to the dharma, so it's the first two of these definitions that are most relevant here - most importantly, the first.

We want to render the dharma relevant to this place and time so that it's accessible and relatable, so that it can be used in day to day life. The dharma is a whole-of-life practice here and now and we want to help people see that. It's not just for people wearing robes or from particular cultures.

Secular dharma is not a 'school' of Buddhism. It has no official organisation or leader, although Stephen Batchelor is leading the way in understanding the Pali canon and spreading the idea of secular dharma. It's more of a grass-roots movement of secular people who've experienced first-hand that the benefits are available regardless of your position on the metaphysical ideas, and who want to share those benefit with others.

The goals are accessibility and benefit for anyone who wants it, including, importantly, those who can't authentically subscribe to the orthodox approaches.

Religion is receding in the Western world, both in terms of prevalence and centrality in people's lives. Here in Australia, the fastest growing religious status is 'none'. Where religion is present in the West, religious tolerance is the aim (although still a work in progress). So for the aim of accessibility, it's most helpful to present the dharma in a non-religious form so that it can also be practised by anyone who subscribes to a religion. Religiosity is no barrier. Secular dharma can be practised by anyone.

So, with no clear boundaries then, what defines the secular approach? I've observed that it's typified by four things:

- **The original suttas of the Pali canon as the North Star:** The use of the *suttas* (recorded dialogues) in the Pali canon as the key source of the teachings, rather than later works. The Pali canon is the earliest version of Gotama's teachings that exists. It does contain some later works but most of the suttas are the earliest recorded teachings. This doesn't preclude embracing later works as part of our practice, but we refer to original suttas in the Pali canon for 'what the Buddha taught'.

- **Openness to all sources:** The use of tools and practices from any source (including orthodox Buddhisms as well as the arts and sciences) with the key criterion that they are helpful.

- **An emphasis on practice:** The emphasis on practical application in everyday real life, not on intellectualising, while recognising an intellectual understanding of the teachings is necessary to an extent. Knowledge is only useful to the extent that it benefits our way of living.

- **Accessibility:** Anyone, anywhere, from any background or life circumstance can practise the dharma.

Of course adapting such a rich body of work carries with it a risk that we could throw out some babies with the bathwater. We don't want to change anything that's central to the understanding and practice of the teachings. This is why the secular approach refers to the earliest version of the teachings possible as its North Star, rather than the many later works which have already been adapted to other cultures and times.

Thankfully this doesn't mean we all have to learn Pali. Several highly knowledgeable scholars and teachers have studied the canon in depth, making the key teachings available to us. (See the Resources section.)

Curiously, some orthodox Buddhists react with anger to the secular approach to the dharma. I say curiously because that reaction itself is prime fodder for dharma practice. Anger (or hatred) is one of the three fires that dharma practice seeks to undermine. As you'll see, dharma practice also involves embracing the idea of impermanence, unreliability, instability in all things - including our ideas and our identities.

The secular approach to the dharma doesn't aim to tear down or denigrate the orthodox approaches. In going back to the earliest source, Batchelor does reject some of the orthodox translations and concepts of the teachings (such as a belief in rebirth being necessary for dharma practice, and the key teachings being seen as 'truths'). I guess it's understandable that these challenges might feel threatening, especially if you've grown up with these beliefs forming part of your world view, your identity, your culture and family history. However the secular approach is by no means a wholesale rejection of all aspects of these rich traditions. Far from it. Indeed there may be times when some of these works and practices could be just what we need.

The Buddha emphasised knowing for ourselves. In my view this is exactly what Batchelor and others are doing by going back to the most original teachings as their primary source. I am profoundly grateful for this: without it I may not have been able to access them as deeply as I have. Indeed I feel deep gratitude to all ancestral Buddhists from the orthodox traditions because without them, we wouldn't have the dharma at all!

The key purpose of this book is to give access to the incredible body of wisdom and life-changing practices within Gotama's teachings for people who would otherwise miss out if orthodox Buddhism were the only door.

It's my hope that readers who might come from orthodox backgrounds can bring to the foreground of their mind the compassion for others that drives my desire to share the dharma in this way.

I hope too, these readers recognise that we are simply doing the very same thing their spiritual ancestors did - adapting the dharma to our own place and time. We are doing this as faithfully to the teachings themselves as possible - looking to these as our North Star, rather than others' interpretations and creations.

Ruffling the feathers of orthodox Buddhists is not the goal. But the dharma is too valuable to let that deter us. I hope these readers see that for many people in the West, it can be either secular dharma or no dharma. A compassionate heart surely wouldn't wish for the latter.

The benefits

The dharma is about experiencing life more fully and honestly, seeing how the patterns of your experience work, and living in a way of greater ease for you and those around you. It's not about detachment in the sense of cutting off from experience. Gotama used several words that can be translated as detachment but none of them have this meaning

Walking this path leads to full human flourishing here and now (no multiple lives needed). It's not spiritual in any metaphysical sense of transcending life, but rather, in the engagement with the great matters of life and death - of living fully. It's a spiritual path in that it leads to a rich, full, deep and vivid engagement with living that creates a sense of grounded uplift. That is, the uplift that comes with freedom from reactivity with your feet on the ground: an uplift that's based on actual, observable, practical, direct experience; on the awe of truly comprehending reality, not concepts, speculations or ideas about escaping it. It's an uplift that brings so much more ease, joy, calm, friendliness, open-heartedness and meaning.

To illustrate how these benefits play out, I'll share some of my stories as we go. (Some are about my athletics experiences but for those uninterested in sport, don't worry, they are human stories, not sport stories.) At the heart of these experiences is a monumental drop in stress and anxiety in all their guises: inadequacy, self-judgment, disappointment, loss, meaninglessness, loneliness to name just a few.

And underpinning this, we lose our fear of our own inner world. Whatever's there is perfectly fine. It may not always be pleasant, but it's all our own unique version of being a human who has the same fundamental needs as everyone else. And as we learn to be more skilful life travellers, we find that none of it is a problem. The whole of life - every single experience - is grist to the mill with dharma practice. It's all food for growth, for insight, for flourishing. Nothing is out of bounds. The path is your whole life!

The ticket to enter this path is the courage and commitment to practise living with unflinching honesty. And one of the truly precious benefits that comes with it is the inspirational and nourishing company of others who are up for the journey. I don't say this lightly - the dharma changed my life. It still does.

What's in store

In this book I move from the general to the specific. Part 1 gives you an orientation to the Buddha, who he was, and what happened to his teachings after his lifetime. I include some common confusions about the teachings, and a high level overview of them. This will give you the big picture - an understanding of the basic teachings and the variety of Buddhisms in context, as well as some guidance on how to start your own dharma practice if you're moved to do that.

Part 2 dives into the detail of the four key planks of Gotama's teachings. I share examples and stories to bring these alive so you can see how both the practices and the benefits of engaging in them show up in today's modern life. And I offer some questions and suggestions in each chapter to help you start applying the dharma in your own life.

In the final chapter, I bring it all together and talk a little about the decision to start walking the dharmic path. For those who'd like another date with the dharma, I offer some further resources at the end of the book.

The extensive Table of Contents will help you learn the concepts or to refresh your memory on any of them. And while I'm keeping the ancient Indian words to a minimum, there are a few you need to know, so there's a short glossary too, covering terms you might not be familiar with.

My sources

Because this book is designed for beginners, I've kept it clean of detailed references. However, in being open about my own lens on the dharma, I'd like to acknowledge some of the more influential sources.

The secular translation and interpretation of the dharma used for this book comes primarily (though not exclusively) from Stephen Batchelor. Considered the unofficial lead pioneer in the Western secular dharma movement, Batchelor spent a decade of his life as a Buddhist monk, first in the Tibetan tradition and then with Zen (or Sŏn as it's known in South Korea where he practised). He speaks with affection about these experiences.

Ultimately, he was moved to leave these traditions and listen to his own intuition, sensing that the dharma could be practised fully without the scaffolds that didn't always sit comfortably with his Western mind. He found this to be true.

Batchelor decided to go back to the earliest form of the teachings that exists - the Pali canon. As you'll discover, the later developments such as Tibetan and Zen Buddhism created their own scriptures based on translations of the teachings but are not simply replicas of the Pali canon in their own language. Indeed, until recently it's possible that many of the different Buddhisms throughout Asia weren't even aware of each other's existence.

Batchelor attempts to know the teachings as clearly as possible before they were infused with local cultures, so that we can do what these cultures so wisely did and infuse it with our own.

Through this book I show how Batchelor's work arrives at some slightly (but important) different interpretations of the teachings from those you'll find in orthodox Buddhist works. The basis for these differences is outlined in detail in his books *After Buddhism: Rethinking the Dharma for a Secular Age* and *Secular Buddhism: Imagining the Dharma in an Uncertain World.*

I share this for those who'd like to do the heavy brain work themselves. (The chapters of After Buddhism that present the evidence upon which he bases his conclusions are a good intellectual work-out and not for the faint of heart.)

His arguments are compelling. Not only are they well justified based on the Pali words themselves, but they make sense to a modern evidence-based mind where more orthodox interpretations don't. Importantly, they also work in practice.

I'm not suggesting more orthodox interpretations don't work for the millions of Buddhists on the planet who practise them. I'm suggesting they may not work for YOU if you have a secular, evidence-based way of understanding the world.

Other key sources include specific books by Anālayo (a Theravadan monk who did his PhD dissertation on the Satipatthana sutta), and Glenn Wallis (a Harvard PhD in Buddhist Studies) as well as many retreats over the years with Insight Meditation teachers such as Gregory Kramer (founder of the Insight Dialogue practice), Jason Siff (also an ex-Theravadan monk and founder of the Recollective Awareness practice) and Rick Hanson (psychologist, author and dharma teacher). These are listed in the Resources section.

I've also been fortunate to know and to have learnt a great deal from some local Insight Meditation teachers including importantly Winton Higgins, as well as Patrick Kearney.

Glossary

dharma	The **teachings** of the Buddha and the **practice** of those teachings.
suttas	**Recordings** of the Buddha's teachings.
dukkha	**Any shade of unpleasant experience** ranging from mild not-quite-rightness, disappointment; from stubbing our toe up to agonising grief and acute pain. Literally: difficult space, or painful space. Generally: the unpleasant.
body–mind	The body and the mind together. They affect each other in so many ways and are inextricably linked. Think of this as **our experiencing system**, the sensory receptacle that registers and also creates our experience.
hungering	The **impulsive desire** to chase more good feelings/sensations and ridding ourselves of unpleasant ones. In orthodox texts this is often called craving. Literally: thirst.
reactivity	Our **thoughts and behaviours** that flow from hungering. The ways we act on the desire to chase pleasant feelings and flee from unpleasant ones. In orthodox texts, this is often called clinging.

nirvana	Literally **quenching, extinguishing, cooling**. The stopping, momentarily or longer, of greed (the desire to gorge on pleasant things), hatred (the desire to push away unpleasant things) and confusion (not seeing/understanding clearly). This results in freedom from hungering and reactivity and sublime experiences of being alive.
BCE	Before the Common Era. This is the secular way to refer to an era rather than Before Christ (BC).
CE	The Common Era. As above rather than AD.

I've tried to minimise the Pali and Sanskrit words (which are generally similar). Where I use them, I explain them. I've used Sanskrit if it's a commonly known spelling of a word like *nirvana*, but I've used the Pali version where it produces a more faithful English pronunciation (e.g. dukkha rather than duhka).

PART 1

AN ORIENTATION

Chapter 1: The Buddha

Who was the Buddha?

Most Buddhist scholars today accept that there was a man named Siddhattha Gotama of the Shakya clan in the Ganges Basin in India. He was commonly referred to as the Buddha, which simply means 'awakened one'. He most likely lived from around 480 to 400 BCE.

Understanding who Gotama was and the circumstance in which he lived is important because it helps us understand his teachings in context. It can help us sort out what might have been said as a spoonful of sugar in order to make the teachings easier to understand and digest. It can also help us to identify which parts of his teachings were original - those at odds with the prevailing assumptions in his time - and so more likely to come from him, rather than those around him or after him.

The traditional view

If you pick a random Buddhist book from the bookshelf, the story you'll read is that Siddhattha Gotama was a prince. You'll read that he lived a cosseted life inside the walls of his father's palace. Then, on a series of outings to a nearby village, he saw four things that changed his life: a sick person, an old person, a dead person, and lastly, a wandering spiritual seeker.

This, so the story goes, was his first experience of suffering. He was so moved by it that he abandoned his royal life (and his wife and new-born child) to go forth as a spiritual seeker himself and discover the answer to the problem of suffering.

So, at the age of 29, he stole away in the middle of the night. He cast aside his royal garments, shaved his head and took up the life of a *samana*, a wandering ascetic.

Ascetics were wandering spiritual seekers, some of whom practised meditation and self-mortification. Self-mortification involved denying oneself pleasures and comforts and inflicting pain for two possible reasons: to transcend attachment to this world; or to try and have their bad karma processed in a job lot.

Gotama, a gifted student, studied with very accomplished meditation masters. He practised this way of life for six years, often eating only a few grains of rice a day. He almost starved to death.

This result was a wake-up call. Through this experience he came to the conclusion that while indulgence (the royal life) wasn't the way to transcend suffering, neither was self-denial. He decided he would sit under a tree and meditate until he figured it out.

So, he sat there for a few weeks meditating. Eventually he gained deep, penetrative insight into how suffering works and the most effective way to deal with it. The traditional account would summarise his discovery as the middle way between indulgence and denial. (It's interesting that the middle way receives such prominence in some orthodox teachings, yet in his 45 years of teaching he only ever mentioned it once - in the first discourse referred to below.)

At first he wasn't sure if he could articulate his insights, but eventually he decided to give it a whirl. So he set off to seek out his three ascetic buddies with whom he'd self-mortified for the past few years, and see if he could communicate what he'd found. He did. They got it. And the wheel of the dharma began to turn.

A modern view

As Stephen Batchelor notes in his book *Confession of a Buddhist Atheist* there is actually very little written about Gotama's life before his awakening. Batchelor set out on a voyage of discovery to try to know this man a little better. He notes that even from the suttas (recorded dialogues) in the Pali canon it's clear that Gotama wasn't a prince at all; he was the son of an elected leader in what's most easily understood in today's parlance as a small republic. He was a member of the warrior caste which made up the ruling council in small republics like his. His father would have been more like one of our state premiers than a king. (In Australia, a state premier is the leader of that state's government.)

It's unclear what he did during his early adult years. He would have been a savvy person as he was exposed to the politics between his father's ruling class and other clans, as well as to the powerful (and sometimes murderous) royal figures who occupied the area. Numerous suttas detail conversations with the regional kings who sought out Gotama's views. Batchelor speculates that he may have even attended the progressive Taxila University, then part of the Persian empire, with some of his contemporaries, where he may have been exposed to ideas and philosophies from different cultures. (He lived at around the same time as Socrates.)

Batchelor points out that the suttas show that the world Gotama occupied was a complex and sometimes dangerous one. Gotama was very engaged with the world, securing patronage and protection for himself and his fellow monks and nuns where possible. He seemed to manage intelligently the need to negotiate support from powerful people, as well as his role as teacher and custodian of his followers. He seemed to have little tolerance for organised religion and was openly critical of it.

Gotama's way of life was very much engaged with the world. He and his followers would spend the few months of the rainy season in sedentary retreat, but when that was over they would wander between places meditating and teaching along the way. Through the suttas we see that he interacted with all sorts of people, from royalty to the town drunk. He owned virtually no stuff (material goods) and referred to the life of the householder as 'cramped and dusty'. It's interesting to contrast this with the illustrious Buddhist temples we see today, full of sedentary monks and nuns.

You can also see this emphasis on engaging with the world through some of the rules in the *vinaya*, the part of the Pali canon containing the rules for monastic life. For example, monks were not allowed to dig soil (to grow their own food). Gotama didn't want his followers shrinking from the world into their own little self-sufficient hermit lives. He wanted them to be interdependent with the villagers and to share the teachings with those around them in a helpful way.

Gotama lived in a society that believed there was a big gap between the spiritual and the everyday - the sacred and the profane (as do many modern religious communities). Life would have been pretty tough in India in the 5th century BCE: the idea of transcending it would have been understandably attractive.

His own clan is likely to have had an animist spiritual view and were known to be sun-worshippers. They would have believed in a similar gap. Brahmanism was taking off in India at the time and was starting to get a foothold in Gotama's region. It too offered a consolation for the difficulties of life: union with Brahma, the godhead; a way out.

In contrast, Gotama taught that spiritual practice is all about this life, indeed these moments that we are inhabiting in this body right now. He taught an approach to living that is an honest confrontation with our experiences of all sorts, an invitation to embrace them, and to learn to live peacefully with the whole thing - the pleasant, the unpleasant and everything in between. His teachings are about confrontation, not consolation; facing and embracing life, not escaping from it.

The traditional fable of Prince Siddhattha is harmless enough. However it doesn't portray the savvy worldliness of the man who is revealed through the suttas.

Chapter 2: The teachings
What is the dharma about?

On one level Gotama's teachings are about how to understand and end unnecessary suffering in your life. The word suffering is a very common translation of the Pali word *dukkha*. As I promised I'll only use ancient Indian words when there is no appropriate English one that reflects the original meaning. I'm mostly going to use the word unpleasantness but this word is at the core of the dharma so I want to be very clear about what I mean.

Every Buddhist tradition centres on some iteration of the *Four Noble Truths*; the heart of both the Noble Truths and of the dharma itself is the concept of dukkha. Because the concept is so core, it's worth taking a moment to understand it.

Dukkha

Most authors I've been exposed to translate dukkha as *suffering*. Other common words are stress, angst, unease, unsatisfactoriness. Let me explain why I'm not going to use these words. Grab a pen and paper and do a little free association exercise. Hold the word suffering in your mind and write down whatever comes into your mind. Next, hold the word *unease* in your mind and do the same.

Chances are the word suffering prompted a list of some pretty unpleasant experiences - loss of loved ones, severe illness or injury, people starving in developing countries perhaps.

I'd guess the word unease prompted much milder and perhaps subtler forms of unpleasantness - perhaps you didn't like the tone of voice your work colleague used with you today.

The word dukkha covers all of these and more. It covers everything from the disappointment that there are no more chocolates in your boxes anymore (as Leonard Cohen sang) to the agony of a mother losing her child. The word unease clearly understates the latter example. Perhaps unpleasantness does too but it strikes me as more generic. A short handy definition could be: anything from the vast range of unpleasant experiences in life.

To really cement your understanding, here's the meaning of the actual Pali word.

Dukkha is a compound word (made up of two words):

du = bad, lousy, crappy, difficult, unpleasant, not good. (The opposite is *su* which means ease)

kha = space (often interpreted as the empty space where an axle would fit into a wheel)

So you could think of it as any difficult or unpleasant space in your experience.

Metaphysics is a distraction

By 'metaphysics' I mean that which is beyond physics (for example ideas of an afterlife, soul, rebirth), ideas that can't be experienced here and now in the world and that we can't know directly.

In one of Gotama's conversations, a monk in his following demands that he tells him the answer to the metaphysical questions that still dog our species. Is there life after death? Do we have a soul? How was the universe created? etc. He tells Gotama that unless he answers these questions, he's going to leave his community of monks.

Gotama gives him a bit of a verbal clip under the ear for missing the point so badly (this was an experienced monk!). He tells him that he teaches how to understand and deal with unpleasantness and does not pretend to address any of these metaphysical questions. In this and other suttas, he pointedly refuses to declare an answer.

The reason for his reprimand was that these questions don't help deal with the very real issue of unpleasantness in this human life of ours. Flourishing in life through changing our relationship to unpleasantness is the core of Gotama's teachings.

But even worse, these questions distract us from the task of living the dharma. In essence he saw metaphysical debates as a waste of time. Indeed in one sutta, Gotama describes intellectual arguments about his teachings as wrong use of the dharma, likening it to grabbing a snake at the wrong end. Not only does it result in harm for ourselves and our relationships with others, but it takes up valuable time that could be devoted to the very real tasks involved in full human flourishing here, now! According to the Buddha, to entertain these metaphysical propositions was as futile as to speculate about the direction in which a fire had departed once it had gone out.

In another well-known sutta, he tells a parable of a man who's been hit with a poisoned arrow. The man refuses to be seen by a doctor until and unless he first knows the name and clan of the man who wounded him, how tall he was, the colour his skin and where he lives, as well as what kind of bow was used to shoot the arrow, what the bowstring and shaft of the arrow were made of, what kind of feathers were on the end of it, and what type of arrow tip it was. Of course he wouldn't find out all of these things and in the meantime he'd die.

Gotama saw metaphysical questions as distractions from what he was on about, that lead us to spend our mental energy on unhelpful questions rather than on the very real project of dealing with unpleasantness and flourishing here and now, which is the very reason why he repeatedly refused to answer such questions.

This is an important point as it draws a clear boundary around what Gotama was and was not teaching. It baffled me a little why that wasn't emphasised more in the dharma books I read as I began my exploration.

It also helps explain why you can hold religious or atheistic beliefs (both equally accept the unknowables) or an agnostic orientation (accepting of uncertainty) and at the same time be able to practise the dharma fully. Such beliefs are unlikely to clash with the essence of Gotama's teachings because his teachings are not about metaphysics.

Tasks to be practised, not Truths to be believed

I started this section by saying that 'on one level Gotama's teachings are about how to understand and end unnecessary suffering in your life'. For religious Buddhists, following the teachings would lead to the earning of merit, which serves as a down-payment on a fortunate rebirth in the next life.

The ultimate goal with this view is to escape the cycle of (re)birth and death all together. For others (some religious, some not) the goal is about the attainment of blissful states which, once well practised, becomes an irreversible state of nirvana.

However Stephen Batchelor challenges these views. He talks about the *Four Tasks* (his version of the Four Noble Truths which I'll explain soon) as a chain of cause and effect themselves, and posits that Gotama presented them in a particular order for a reason.

The main point of the dharma, he suggests, is full human flourishing in this life, rather than transcending human life either now or in imagined future rebirths, or attaining some permanent state of bliss for ourselves. He refers to one of the few suttas where Gotama spoke of his awakening. He likened it to someone finding an ancient path to a forgotten city, whose task was to gather the people with the skills and resources to help this community flourish once again.

Batchelor points to the outcome being engagement with life in a different way, rather than some blissful or superhuman state, let alone another life. It's about know-how for living now, not know-ledge of some escape route. In this scenario, becoming skilful with unpleasantness, the difficult spaces in our lives here and now, is central to the practice.

Some interpretation of the Four Noble Truths forms the foundational architecture of the dharma in every approach. I'll explain these in a moment, but first there's a very important point to be aware of regarding the nature of these 'truths'.

The four planks of the dharma are not like commandments bestowed from a god, that carry with them an expectation that they will be believed much less swallowed whole. Batchelor points out that KR Norman one of the world's foremost philologists (and an expert in the group of ancient languages that includes Pali) concludes that the original sutta did not contain the words 'noble truth' at all.

From Batchelor:

> "The term 'noble truth' is so much taken for granted, that we fail to notice its polemical, sectarian and superior tone. All religions maintain that what they and they alone teach is both 'noble' and 'true.' This is the kind of rhetoric used in the business of religion. It is easy to imagine how over the centuries after the Buddha's death his followers, as part of the inter-sectarian one-upmanship of ancient India, made increasingly elevated claims about the superiority of their teacher's doctrines, which resulted in the adoption of the expression 'noble truth' to privilege and set apart the dharma from what their competitors taught."

Whatever the truth about the 'noble truths', the question I find most valuable is:

How does this help?

There are more useful ways of referring to the four key planks of Gotama's teachings that help avoid the trap of adopting them as doctrine. I find Batchelor's argument compelling, and he refers to them simply as the Four Tasks.

I like to add the descriptor *Great* as it seems to be helpful in two ways. It reminds me that I'm attempting something big (to shift my experience of life!) and difficult. So when I fall off the wagon, which I do frequently, it helps prevent me from giving up. What 'great big' achievement was ever made smoothly and easily?!

It's also great in the sense that it leads to wonderful things. The word *noble* may not have been in the original titles, but this endeavour is indeed noble. It leads to a much kinder, more compassionate, wise, aware way of living that inflicts much less harm on ourselves and others. If that's not a 'great' aim, I don't know what is!

Rather than dogma, think of the Four Great Tasks as enquiry questions to be tested out, as invitations to do something if you have the curiosity and the courage. Gotama never asked nor expected people to believe what he said just because he said it. He encouraged people to test out ideas fully against their own experience in order to assess their veracity.

Know through direct experience

In one well-known sutta, Gotama addresses the inhabitants of a town called Kalama. As this town occupies a crossroads, it has many travellers passing through including itinerant teachers (samanas), each claiming their own views to be right and everyone else's to be wrong. (Some things haven't changed much over the millennia have they?)

The Kalamas had heard that Gotama had quite a reputation but knew little else about him. They presented him with their bewilderment at all the contradictory messages they were getting. Gotama congratulated them on pinpointing a very real problem (the difficulty in knowing what to believe) and proceeded to suggest how they might select what to take on board.

First, he listed a bunch of sources NOT to rely on. That's not to say to throw them out as unreliable, but don't accept something just because it comes from:

- unconfirmed reports from other people
- traditions handed down from the past
- hearsay
- written scriptures
- logical reasoning (which can often lead to absurd conclusions)
- inferential logic (e.g. all the swans I've seen are white therefore all swans are white)
- reflection on reasons
- acceptance of a speculative view after pondering it
- the impression of competence from the speaker
- someone you consider to be your teacher.

The only test you can rely on is your own experience, Gotama said. Does a particular teaching, when put fully into practice lead to a reduction in unpleasantness, the cooling or quenching of reactivity, to wholesome benefit, contentment, equanimity? If it does, adopt it. If it doesn't, drop it. This is what I mean by the question: how does it help?

This is one of the reasons meditation is so important to dharma practice - we need to develop our observation skills of our own experience - our experiential acuity if you like. Without this, we won't notice the many causes and effects at play.

In modern Western societies where our lives play out on fast-forward, this is very relevant. Something I've noticed in my own practice is that speed and mindfulness don't go together - it's very hard to have both. To be present to our experience in any detail, most of us need to slow down. This is because our attention is a finite resource.

To this end, I've invented an imaginary organisation named PAR, which stands for People Against Rushing. To become a member, all you have to do is to hold the intention to slow down. This has practical implications for things like the time you leave for appointments, and how much you pack into a day. I've found the impacts to be wholly beneficial. Feel free to sign up! 😊 (You can download a free PAR card from the Mindfulness Tools page on my website.)

Recognising the wise

For the sake of completeness, it's worth mentioning that in addition to testing things fully against our own experience, Gotama also encouraged people to listen to 'the wise', that is, anyone you recognise as informed, level-headed and with good judgment. In another famous sutta he elaborates on how one can tell whether a teacher is worth listening to.

In this instance two young Brahmins were discussing the inconsistencies between the teachings of their respective Brahmin priests, each arguing that his particular priest was right. Again, having heard of Gotama's reputation and knowing he was in the neighbourhood, they decided to find him and ask his view of how to decide which teachers to believe.

Gotama used questioning to help the young fellows assess whether their teachers possessed the qualities of the God they claimed to represent. Again, he was emphasising here the key question: does it help? That is, do your teachers' instructions appear to help them achieve the very things they're on about? Specifically he asked if they were:

- not wrapped up in possessions (versus wrapped up in possessions)
- composed (versus ill-tempered)
- gracious (versus antagonistic)

- honest (versus corrupt)

- compliant (versus domineering).

In reflecting, the young Brahmins realised both of their teachers were wrapped up in possessions, ill-tempered, antagonistic, corrupt and domineering. So the key question is: does the teacher embody the qualities that their teachings claim to produce? Do they walk the talk?

In the case of the dharma, a credible teacher would embody the principle of non-harm that runs through the *Eightfold Path*, and often display at least some of the following qualities, the *Seven Factors of Awakening*:

- Mindfulness/Awareness

- Curiosity (about your experience using the dharma as your lens)

- Energy

- Delight

- Tranquillity

- Mental integration (consistency of mental direction)

- Equanimity.

Know-how versus know-ledge

The sutta in which Gotama first articulates these insights is one of the few where he talks about his awakening. In this he says that until he'd been able to communicate the insights, his awakening wasn't complete. Importantly, he also said that knowing the Great Tasks isn't enough. For each of the four, we have to know it and practise it until we've accomplished it in order to awaken.

So the Four Great Tasks summarise the core of what Gotama realised through his awakening. The insights describe the way we make a real mess for ourselves with unpleasantness or the difficult spaces in life and offer us the challenge of dismantling our mess-making habits.

This allows us to encounter a peaceful and joyful way of living. Each Task contains something to understand, something to practise and something to achieve. The emphasis is on practical challenge rather than intellectual 'truth'. That is, the dharma is more practical know-how for flourishing in life, rather than know-ledge to be consumed intellectually. Indeed I've noticed that people who are only willing to engage their intellect tend to give up, disappointed that it didn't change their life.

The Four Great Tasks / The Four Noble Truths

So let's get down to business. What are the Four Tasks? A Secular Buddhist will give you a slightly different answer to the average religious Buddhist, so both answers are summarised below.

I'm being a bit glib referring to an 'average religious Buddhist' because there is probably no such individual given the vast array of religions that have sprung from the dharma (see Chapter 4: Is Buddhism a Religion?).

However, when approaching it for the first time I think it's useful to have some broad summaries to help structure learning. To this end, I've written this overview of the key planks of the dharma and the major differences between more common orthodox approaches and the emerging secular approach.

Also bear in mind as you read it that the secular description is not the exclusive domain of Secular Buddhism. For example, much of it would be shared by some Zen Buddhists. In the remaining chapters my primary task is explaining the secular approach, so I want to orient you in the big picture, to the way this differs from the more common religious approaches you might encounter. Hopefully this will help avoid confusion when you come across the much more common religious writings, podcasts and other resources.

The second part of this book gives a lot more detail, but to start with, here's an overview.

Traditional view

First Noble Truth: The truth of suffering (life is suffering)

Because everything in life is impermanent, unstable and unreliable, everything contains suffering. The definition of suffering is:

- birth
- sickness
- old age
- death
- being parted from things we love
- being thrown together with things we don't like
- not getting what we want

- our whole vulnerable psycho-physical condition as humans.

This list covers the entirety of the human experience, which is why it's frequently represented as 'life is suffering'.

Second Noble Truth: The truth of suffering's cause (suffering is caused by craving)

We crave for unpleasant experiences to stop, and we crave for pleasant experiences to continue. It's this craving for things to be different that causes our suffering.

Third Noble Truth: The truth of the cessation of suffering (it's possible to stop craving, therefore stop suffering)

If we can let go of the craving for things to be different, we let go of suffering, and attain a permanent state of liberation from the cycle of death and re-birth.

Fourth Noble Truth: The truth of the Noble Eightfold Path (the path to awakening)

If we live life in accordance with the Eightfold Path, we find nirvana (usually translated as liberation). The eight 'folds' are:

- Right View
- Right Intention
- Right Action
- Right Speech
- Right Livelihood
- Right Effort
- Right Mindfulness
- Right Concentration.

Secular view

Because secular dharma is an approach to practice, not an institution there is no officially sanctioned version of the key teachings. What offer you here is a description that, to me, is both faithful to the secular understanding of the teachings (in line with Batchelor's reading of them easy to remember, and helpful in a practical way.

First Task: See, expect and accept unpleasantness

Unpleasantness is a part of life. Our challenge is to see where it arises, accept it as part of our experience, expect it as part of our daily life, and get to know intimately how it feels and how it works - to embrace it along with the pleasant stuff.

Second Task: Dismantle reactivity

When unpleasantness arises, so does the impulsive hunger for things to be pleasant. Our challenge is to dismantle the automatic reaction of scrambling for the pleasant things to last forever and the unpleasant things to go away.

Third Great Task: Fully experience non-reactivity

Notice, recognise, experience and understand intimately the state of non-reactivity (nirvana) and the truly wonderful experiences that flow from it.

Fourth Great Task: Walk the Eightfold Path

Eight important facets of life help us live the dharma. The challenge is to pay attention to them, notice our choices and their consequences, genuinely explore the insights Gotama shared about certain choices, and choose wisely. The eight folds are almost the same as in the traditional view, but without the polemical 'right' prefix:

- Understanding
- Intention
- Action
- Speech
- Livelihood
- Effort
- Mindfulness
- Mental integration.

What similarities and differences do you notice between these two versions of the four important planks of Gotama's teachings? There are some similarities such as the recognition and acceptance of unpleasantness, the importance of undermining our reactive habit of hungering (craving) for pleasant things to continue and unpleasant ones to stop, and our reactive habits of trying to bring this about (clinging). The importance of mindfulness is central in both, and they both contain an almost-identical list of eight areas to focus on in life.

As you'll see, other commonalities are the recognition that everything arises only from conditions being right for it, the importance of seeing clearly the impermanence of things, and breaking out of the delusions that pleasure can bring indelible happiness, as well as fixed ideas about our identities. Orthodox Buddhism and secular dharma spring from the same well.

There are also some important differences to notice:

- The traditional version is a series of statements, or truth claims to be believed, whereas the secular version is a series of tasks or challenges with a focus on practice rather than belief.

- The traditional version portrays human life as unpleasant, whereas the secular version portrays unpleasantness as an integral part of human life, but not its totality. 'Life has difficult spaces', not 'life is a difficult space'.

- The traditional version involves a metaphysical proposition (re-birth), whereas the secular version emphasises Gotama's focus on lived experience here and now.

- The traditional version contains terms that tend to privilege or elevate the teachings (e.g. 'noble' truths, 'right' view) which the secular version doesn't.

- The traditional version offers a complete escape from unpleasantness, which the secular version doesn't.

Awakening

Awakening is the experiencing of life free from reactivity. This yield a viscerally different way of receiving life infused with much more contentment, joy, energy, warmth, friendliness and equanimity.

You probably know the term nirvana - that's the state of awakening It literally means 'quenching', 'extinguishment' or 'cooling', although it often represented as 'liberation' which is what arises with this quenching What is quenched? The 'three fires':

- greed - desire to hoard or prolong pleasant experience

- hatred - aversion to anything unpleasant

- confusion - misperceiving how life works, especially in relation to happiness and wellbeing versus sorrow and strife.

With awakening these impulses simply stop driving us and what the arises is a different experience of life – we're less thrown around by i more open, friendly, joyful, peaceful, more able to greet calmly whatever our life entails.

This is an area where you'll encounter a difference between some of the orthodox Buddhisms and the secular approach. The former sees awakening as release from the cycle of (re)birth and death. The latter sees it as a way of experiencing life, heeding Gotama's very clear view that metaphysical issues such as life after death were irrelevant to his teachings.

Related to this, orthodox Buddhisms see awakening as the complete end of suffering, whereas the secular approach sees it as the complete end of reactivity. That is, the end to our compulsive chasing of pleasure and avoiding of non-pleasure and all the mess we make for ourselves by doing this. It also includes the sublime experiences of life that arise when we quench the fires that drive that chasing.

We'll explore this concept of awakening in more detail in the Third Great Task.

Karma

Karma literally means 'action'. Practically, it refers to the process of intentional action and consequence. Many teachings from the traditional era of Buddhism interpret this as a kind of merit system where you perform good deeds (e.g. for lay people, donating to Buddhist temples) to earn 'merit' which then positions you well for a fortunate rebirth in the next life. A Buddhist teacher I know, Winton Higgins, refers to this as the 'merit-go-round'.

As with the concept of rebirth, there is no requirement to believe in this concept of karma. In fact my experience has shown me that this idea of transactional karma, where we do X and receive Y later on, actually has a negative effect on my practice.

Once when I was listening to a talk by a Buddhist monk, my curiosity led me to experiment with the impact of holding such a belief. Gotama encourages us to test ideas out fully. So I imagined how I would feel, and what I would be motivated to do, if it were really true that the intentional action I engage in now were to dictate my rebirth in future lives.

The answer came to me quickly. The first thing I felt was fear, somewhat akin to the fear of punishment in Catholicism. What if I hadn't done enough to secure a fortunate rebirth? What if I get reborn as a beggar on the streets of India? Holy moly, I'd better get out there and start doing some more good deeds!

Why? Not because I feel compassion for others but for my own good fortune! Something I love about the dharma is that our selves are seen as equally deserving of compassion as anyone else, so self-compassion is a worthy movement of the heart. But I found that this overshadowed compassion for others, almost rendering it unnecessary.

Intention is a very important concept in the dharma as we'll see. So much so that it's embedded in the Eightfold Path, a key plank of the teachings. When I tested out the idea of karma as a merit-earning act, I found that the intentions for any supposedly kind act shifted from compassion for others to safety for myself. It wasn't necessary to open to the shared experience of being human. That seems at odds with the teachings.

The other thing I noticed was that the catalyst for action shifted from internal to external. Rather than acting as a response to the inner experience of compassion, my actions would be sparked by fear of the unknown algorithm within the black box of karma distribution.

Traditional Buddhist teachings say there is no 'being' that distributes karmic reward and punishment, it's just the way the world works. I can't swallow this one, and besides, there are many instances where appropriate reward and punishment are not dealt out for actions. I see this belief as simply a relic of Brahmanism's influence on Buddhism after Gotama's death.

Another negative effect I've witnessed as a result of believing in the karmic merit-go-round is a distinct lack of compassion for people experiencing hardship. Instead of empathy, there can be an attitude of coldness because the afflicted person is simply experiencing 'their karma': 'Joe Bloggs was attacked in his home and stabbed three times. Oh well, that's his karma'.

The attitude is that it's some form of immanent (inherent) justice and he earned his misfortune. This is utterly at odds with the emphasis on compassion and kindness in the teachings.

This understanding of karma as the cause of all things is also ignorant. Gotama was clear about the fact that karma was only one of many causes. Others included biological and physiological factors as well as sheer luck.

The idea of karma has already gained a place in Western society, and generally refers to the idea that 'what goes around comes around'. In my view this is actually a good way to think about it.

Setting your intentions in a certain way has all sorts of knock-on effects. Your intention will affect what you pay attention to, the choices you make both big and small, the way you behave, the way you speak to and deal with other people, whom you speak to, the things you talk about, the attitudes you express, what you remember, and more. All these things affect the people and environment around you.

It's in this way that I see our intentions and actions bringing consequences home to roost, not through any 'secret', nor through some mysterious metaphysical accounting system.

A little more on the Four Great Tasks

A virtuous cycle

In one sense the Four Great Tasks are sequential. By truly knowing unpleasantness - the difficult spaces - we see more clearly how it works and what causes it, and we expect and accept it. We realise the futility of rejecting our humanness and all the carry-on we engage in to reactively feed our hungers as a means of always feeling good. We get over these reactive habits. It's like a child who finally learns that throwing tantrums doesn't get her what she wants. We finally see that the carry-on actually makes things worse. So we just drop it.

Once we really see the ineffectiveness of our reactive hunger-feeding strategies the hungering urges dissipate, and we can know more fully the peaceful and joyful states that naturally arise when reactivity drops away. Then everything changes: the way we think, speak, work, and act; our effort; our level of awareness; and the nature of our focus.

In an experiential sense however, the Four Great Tasks are not sequential. On a day-to-day basis, we are in a constant flow between these things, there are two-way feedback loops all over the place, and what is prominent at any moment is unpredictable. So while the tasks feed into each other sequentially, any part of the Four Great Tasks could be front and centre of our attention at any time.

Cultivating the folds of the Eightfold Path also helps us achieve the first three Great Tasks: embracing unpleasantness, dismantling reactivity, and fully experiencing non-reactivity. A similar mutuality also occurs in the field of psychology. Cognitive psychology shows us that we can change from the inside out. By changing the way we think and perceive, we can change the way we feel and behave. Behavioural psychology shows us that we can also change from the outside in. Changing our behaviour can change the way we feel and think. The Eightfold Path gives us guidance for both types of change.

The Eightfold Path and the first three Great Tasks are intertwined in a virtuous cycle. Rather than approaching them as truth claims, understand them and test them out fully yourself.

Chapter 3: Some common confusions

Does the dharma state that all of life is suffering?

No. Indeed in one sutta Gotama was asked this directly and stated that there are three fundamental aspects of life: unpleasantness, ease, and quenching (dukkha, sukha and nirvana). The dharma is about embracing the whole of the human experience, including the pleasant bits. There's lots more on this under the First Great Task.

Is the dharma just meditation or mindfulness?

No. Mindfulness is a central and an essential practice that runs through all of the teachings but it's not the whole kit and caboodle by any stretch of the imagination.

Gotama taught that by applying mindfulness to all aspects of our experience using the lens of his teachings, we see how this being-human process works. Doing this to the point where we have penetrative insights about our experience releases us from reactivity, and gradually produces a different way of being in the world.

This is an important point because mindfulness seems to be all the rage these days. However, mindfulness programs frequently offer the benefits of full dharma practice as the result of simply practising meditation for 20 minutes a day. This is false advertising.

Spending 20 minutes a day on the meditation cushion will produce a bit more calm and a bit less stress, as well as some more awareness of your experience. Those are good things. But if you want the full benefits, you've got to walk the path, and that involves much more than meditation. I haven't seen those disclaimers anywhere in the mindfulness training brochures!

Dharma practice also involves an earnest engagement with an ethical way of living. The core principles running through this ethical framework are non-harm and awareness. There are no Christianity-style commandments. Dharma practice involves looking closely at the choices we make in our lives on a day-to-day basis and paying attention to the consequences of those choices.

While Gotama did outline eight specific areas of life that are central to the awakening process (the Eightfold Path), they are not rules to be followed in order to please a metaphysical being. They are areas Gotama identified as having a powerful impact on awakening.

Full dharma practice involves experimenting with and paying close attention to these areas in our lives. Mindfulness is important because it helps us pay attention better, and make more deliberate, mindful, ethical choices. However it, by itself, is only a part of the picture.

Could mindfulness do the trick without Gotama's teachings? Theoretically yes. Gotama himself is an example of that. He gained the insights he did without a Buddha to guide him. However this is extremely difficult and it's extremely unlikely that you or I will manage it, especially living a modern life of busy-ness as we do. Are you dedicated enough to discovering these insights yourself that you'll devote years of your life, full time, to meditation and spiritual practice? Probably not.

So we have the advantage of Gotama having shared his insights on how being human works, and how to stop making a mess of it. As we contemplate these insights and test them out with increasing mindfulness of our experience, our way of seeing and receiving the world changes.

Ultimately, awakening is a process that helps us towards a less reactive and more peaceful, kind, loving way of life - not because we 'should' in order to be a good Buddhist, but because we see for ourselves the consequences of our choices. These insights lead us to **want** to make kinder choices.

This process involves seeing and integrating into our life the reality of the human experience. Thanks to our modern lives, the chances are low that we'd hit upon all of these insights on our own, even with a regular mindfulness practice.

It's also worth mentioning that sitting meditation is only one form of mindfulness. Not only are there other forms of meditation (walking meditation, lying down meditation) but mindfulness is a general practice. The goal is to be mindful (aware) all the time no matter what you're doing. You can substitute the word 'awareness' as a pretty good alternative.

What's the link between meditation and the dharma?

Meditation is important for two key reasons. They neatly correspond with the two key elements of dharma practice: serenity and insight.

Serenity: When we subject our body–mind to a constant stream of stimulation, it's constantly stirred up. We are sensitive creatures - quite literally - responding continuously to the stream of information being met by our sensorium (our body–mind) which is the mechanism for our existence in this world. When we leave no spaces in-between bouts of stimulation, especially the mental stimulation that's involved with mental effort, we end up wired, edgy, and reactive.

Importantly, in this state our capacity to make values-based, considered decisions is diminished. What Gotama discovered experientially has been supported through psychological research. In his excellent book *Thinking Fast and Slow* Daniel Kahneman, a Nobel Prize winning researcher and author, describes two decision making systems that are constantly in play in our body–minds.

System 1 is the more intuitive, easy, fast-responding system that relies on associations and 'gut feel'. System 2 is the more effortful, deliberate, considered system that makes more thoughtful assessments. If we're trying to change our reactive habits, we need the second system at our disposal. If we're over-taxing our body–minds from dawn to dusk, it's much harder to access it. It runs out of energy.

It's also the case that when we experience a 'negative event' in our day, we need time to let the physiological effects of this dissipate. Let's say someone criticised our work in front of our colleagues. For many people this would feel threatening to our identity as a competent, respect-worthy person. On a physiological level that sense of threat is coursing through our body in the form of hormones like adrenaline and cortisol.

It takes time for this to be processed and leave our body. (Interestingly, exercise is the fastest way to process it, so if you're stressed, don't skip that gym session!) If we rush off to the next meeting before these physiological ripple-effects have dissipated, we start that meeting already on high alert. We're more likely to interpret interactions from that meeting as threatening and we're more likely to react defensively rather than respond helpfully.

In short, without the touchstone of serenity in our day we're more likely to cause harm to ourselves and others - the antithesis of the dharma.

Insight: Intense busy-ness and speed are two features that infuse our modern lives. Both are enemies of clear seeing. We have a finite attentional bandwidth; the more we rush, the less we can notice about any given moment.

This is really obvious in athletics. Any action that's done at speed is very hard to learn because it's so difficult to pay attention to the detail of what you're doing. For example, learning to do block starts can take a lot of time because it's performed so quickly. Learning the sprint hurdles is the same.

When I'm trying to improve on these activities, the best I can do is hold in mind my intention to do something, let's say that's to stay low over the hurdles, and then go. Because there is so much going on in any given second, my attentional bandwidth simply isn't big enough to take in the detail.

With sprint hurdles, in the space of about 1.2 seconds, I land after the previous hurdle, regain my balance, accelerate again, turn the legs over fast, judge my distance from the next hurdle, hold my balance for take off, ensure the lead leg is bent, and whip the trailing leg through quickly. This all happens so fast I can't attend to it in detail.

It's exactly the same in daily life. If we pack our diary full and set ourselves tight deadlines for things, we'll rush through our day so quickly we won't have the attentional bandwidth to notice anything but the essentials of getting through it. Dharma practice requires us to get to know our own experience, our patterns of reacting to things on a detailed level: mind activity, emotions, body sensations. Ultimately we want to see these things as soon as they arise.

This points to the value of retreats in dharma practice. On retreat we're removing much of the day-to-day stimulation of our lives. We have our meals taken care of, we have no family, work or domestic obligations and we spend several hours a day meditating. In my experience these conditions are conducive to insights about my own process - my patterns and habits that affect my experience of life.

Cultivating our mindfulness muscle involves simply repeating the process of bringing our attention to what's going on, both inside of us and outside of us. At first we might find that we only remember to do this once or twice in an entire meditation sitting. Maybe not until the very end when it's over. But as we practise the habit of paying attention, the mind takes that route more and more often.

A really helpful catalyst for doing it is paying attention to the body, because that reflects what's going on in the mind. In my early days of meditating, I'd use obvious body sensations as little flags to remind me to pay attention to my experience rather than just being in it.

Tension in the body is a common one - I notice that my shoulders are up around my ears, or my jaw is clenched or my brow is in a frown, or it might even be a smile, or I'd notice an elevated feeling of energy. I'd take that cue to shift my attention from being lost in whatever was causing the sensation, to ask myself gently, 'What's going on here?'

Meditation is not just sitting meditation: it's awareness generally in all of our daily activities. But a dedicated meditation (sitting, walking, lying down) is an important part of this.

The fact that Gotama continued to practise it right up until his death is instructive. It's in the nature of our body–minds to be affected in the ways I've described here. That's just the creature that we are. Arguably our modern lives involve an even greater barrage of stimulation than in Gotama's time. That suggests meditation is even more important.

Does the dharma teach passivity - accepting rather than acting?

No. It teaches the value of accepting and then responding out of calmness, creativity and an intention of non-harm. Our usual habit is to resist reality, create a big stink about the fact that things haven't gone the way we wanted, and to react impulsively fuelled by that angst.

Accept and respond: don't resist and react.

The truth is that in that reactive state we are stuck in a rut. We don't have access to the full range of our creative capabilities, and we are likely to damage ourselves and our relationships by moving to action. It's a really unpleasant way to live life.

The dharma teaches us to accept and respond creatively from values, rather than resist and react impulsively. It's not about passively sitting by or being a Buddhist doormat. At times, being forthright or firm can be the most appropriate response. But when this comes from a place of awareness and compassion it's very different to reactivity.

Isn't avoiding pain (the unpleasant) good?

A common question that comes up is, 'What's wrong with wanting to avoid pain? Isn't that natural? Isn't that how we survived as a species?'

The avoid-pain/seek-pleasure principle is indeed at the heart of survival for most animals on the planet. And from a Darwinian point of view where keeping your genes in the gene pool was the goal of existence, this served us well. Seeking sweet (energy-rich) foods, and, in particular, sex were central to keeping us alive and breeding. Avoiding pungent smelling foods and physical pain were equally important.

However in the modern Western world, few of us still live under the law of the jungle where physical survival and procreation are our primary goals. Most of us have safe homes, enough food, protection from the elements, and can procreate if we wish. Indeed even those whose bodies wouldn't naturally procreate can do so with the help of technologies like IVF.

In our modern developed world 'the game' has changed. Physical survival is no longer such an issue. Now, psycho–social survival takes pre-eminence for most of us. What I mean by that is having a healthy psychological, emotional and social life. These are intricately linked.

Like hunger and thirst, the need to belong and be connected with others is a fundamental part of being human. It's part of our genetic heritage. In an evolutionary sense, belonging was directly linked to physical survival. If you were cast out of your tribe, the likelihood that you'd survive at all, let alone successfully procreate, would take a nose-dive.

It's an important point. Belonging and connectedness are not 'nice to-haves': they are deeply embedded in our DNA. Indeed most of the unique parts of the human brain are involved in social processing of some kind.

I'd like to suggest that in our modern world where the basics are taken care of, this need for connection is the most common source of unpleasantness. Test it for yourself. Jot down the things that have been stressing you most in the past month. How many of them are linked t physical survival? How many are essentially linked to what others think of you; whether they like or approve of or respect you, or whether you belong and are accepted? If you're working hard to earn a lot of money, is it because you fear you won't have enough to eat or anywhere safe to shelter? Probably not. It's more likely to be about being successful either financially or through your achievements. This is usually about your reputation or image in others' eyes.

There's a good chance that most of your stressors are in the second category - they are to do with how you are seen by others. This is meaningful because our need for connection is at stake. The pain springs from emotional turmoil, not physical harm.

That probably makes sense to you; however, here's the hitch. With few exceptions, the avoid pain/seek pleasure principle doesn't work with psycho–social survival. Most of our emotional pain is based on faulty beliefs about our reality, and the more we avoid looking at the processes at work inside of us, the more those processes scare us.

This is the pain paradox. In order to flourish psycho–socially, we need to reverse our genetic predisposition to avoid pain and seek pleasure. We need to stop running from the unpleasant, turn around, and look it in the eye.

This is central to Gotama's teaching. If we are to get intimate with unpleasantness and stop desperately hungering for things to be different, we need to undo our habitual reaction to it. We need to learn to approach it with gentleness and curiosity rather than flee from it, deny it, or block it out.

The ironic thing about unpleasantness is that 'leaning into the discomfort', into the difficult spaces, is actually the more helpful response. 'Leaning in' doesn't mean acting in a way that makes it worse. It just means directing our attention and curiosity to it, not fleeing from it and discharging its energy in an unhelpful way by fighting it, denying or avoiding it or falling in a heap hoping for rescue. Gotama's teachings are a great guide for this 'leaning in'.

Is yoga a part of the dharma?

No, although they both come from the same time (approximately 5th century BCE) and cultural and spiritual birthplace, India. Physical yoga practice is often used as a movement meditation on Buddhist retreats and programs, and they both share the practice of sitting meditation (which was already well developed by the time Gotama came along). The earliest accounts of yoga practice actually occur in Buddhist suttas.

Yoga is also part of a belief-based religion, Hinduism, which encourages devotion to gurus and belief in the *atman* or true inner self, which is essentially a little piece of the transcendent Brahman (the supreme self). As you'll see, one of Gotama's core insights was that there is no enduring 'self'. The dharma does not have to be interpreted as a recipe for transcending this life in order to attain another sort of life, but rather as a recipe for living the life we have differently, in a far more creative, free, joyful and peaceful way. The differences are quite fundamental.

Is the Dalai Lama a Buddha?

It's difficult to get a straight answer to this question. I've even asked a friend who was a Tibetan monk working with the Dalai Lama. It seems that most Tibetan Buddhists would say yes, but then they'd probably say that about any of their teachers - it's kind of the done thing.

One issue that often prompts this question is the fact that the Dalai Lama eats meat which is part of the traditional Tibetan diet. This is clearly harmful. He did stop doing this at one point in response to pleas from many practitioners, as his choice on this front influences many other Buddhists and the result is a great deal of harm for animals. However, his personal Tibetan physician advised him to resume doing so for health reasons.

Nevertheless, the Dalai Lama certainly seems to embody many of the qualities that are hallmarks of the awakening process (more on those later) and Gotama emphasised this as an important indicator of a teacher's credibility. Indeed I heard a well-known American dharma teacher Jack Kornfield speculate that people go to see the Dalai Lama to experience his laughter more than to hear the teachings. Joyfulness or delight is a hallmark of awakening and he exudes this despite the immense difficulties he's faced.

Why are some depictions of the Buddha fat?

It can be a bit confusing to learn that the dharma has a focus on having a healthy, reality-based relationship to pleasure, and then to come across images of a morbidly obese Buddha.

As it turns out, the depictions of a fat Buddha aren't Gotama at all. They are representations of a Chinese man named Budai or Butai who lived in 10th century CE. He acted a bit like Santa Claus, asking people what their needs were and producing whatever they needed out of the sack he carried around - a bit like the Room of Requirement in the Harry Potter series. Some stories claim he was a Buddha in their midst. But these are not depictions of Siddhattha Gotama.

Is there one 'right' way to meditate?

No. In fact Gotama spent very little of his teaching time instructing people in meditation. In the most significant sutta in which he does do this (the Satipatthana Sutta) he gave a whole range of aspects of experience that could be contemplated in meditation: body sensations including the breath as well as all body movements and functions; feeling tones; the mind; hindrances that we encounter; different clusters of experience such as our reactions to things and conscious thoughts; our sense spheres and their contact with the environment; the 'awakening factors'.

Clearly, these instructions included mindfulness of bodily activities, but these are just some of the many parts of our experience he mentioned. It's not exclusively about sitting on a cushion feeling the movement of the breath. Any meditation teacher who tells you that mindfulness of breathing is the only 'correct' or worthwhile meditation technique is making it up.

Generally speaking, meditation techniques fall into two buckets: insight and serenity, the two elements needed for walking the path. Concentration practices fall broadly into the 'serenity' bucket because they calm the mind by focusing it. This includes breath meditation, guided meditations, reciting mantras - anything that deliberately focuses the mind.

The practices that fall into the 'insight' bucket are those that help us see our experience clearly. These include much more fluid practices where you let your mind do what it wants but you bring awareness to it. They also include simply 'noting' or 'labelling' what kind of thoughts you're having. This way you see your own patterns, how they come and go, what leads to them arising and what leads to their disappearance.

The contemplations that Gotama suggested also yield insights that help shift the way we see, receive and experience the world. Insight Meditation is not one specific practice, but rather a generic name for practices that are designed to yield insight.

Do I have to believe in rebirth or reincarnation to practise the dharma?

No. This leads to another important boundary. Gotama was once asked if he was omniscient (all-knowing) and declared he wasn't. Like us, he was a child of his time (he lived in the 5th century BCE) so indeed there's every chance he believed that we are, in some sense, reborn, even if there is no stable entity to be reborn. There's a good chance he also believed the earth was flat.

In some of his chats with people, Gotama referred to heaven and hell realms, rebirth and gods (although gods in this paradigm were more like sprites in premodern Western folklore, and inferior to realised human beings), and devas (other god-like supernatural beings). He spoke of these things as if he believed in them.

So, either he was employing a language and paradigm that his dialogue partners would understand and accept, or he genuinely believed them. They were unquestioned assumptions in his time, a bit like gravity is an unquestioned assumption in ours. Imagine if someone on earth today tried to teach in a way that contravened the existence of gravity! Their audience would dwindle quickly.

It's also worth knowing that in one of Gotama's briefest suttas he describes to his fellow monks and nuns the entirety of the human experience, which did not involve extra-sensory perception of any kind. In essence, he declares that the entire human experience is made up of our six senses and their contact with the world. That is, the five senses we all know, plus the mind, which Gotama also considered to be a sense. If I go by my own experience, that leaves gods and devas in the 'mind' category - nothing more than products of our minds.

It's important to know that not one of Gotama's teachings **require us** to believe in these metaphysical concepts. Indeed if we follow one of his core teachings - that we should test things out fully for ourselves to know if they are true - then I have to conclude that these things probably do not exist other than as thoughts, as I have never encountered them through any of the other senses.

Other teachings too, logically contravene concepts such as literal rebirth. For example the core teaching of 'not-self': that we do not have a fixed, independent, enduring identity that is 'me'. Rather, we are more like a dynamic process, a momentary experience that is always changing according to the conditions inside and outside us. This would seem to preclude the idea of 'me' being reborn as it would require that some part of me is fixed and enduring and independent of conditions (such as breathing air).

In a dialogue I attended between Stephen Batchelor and a Theravadin Buddhist monk, Venerable Sujato, inevitably this question arose and was posed to Sujato: what was the mechanism for rebirth if there is no enduring self? Sujato comes across as an intelligent, educated and down-to-earth person and I was genuinely intrigued to hear his answer.

He said, 'Because everything is energy of course!'

I was SO disappointed! I've heard this vague pseudo-scientific statement used to explain everything from auras to ghosts, never with any detailed explanation of how the process works. At best, I need to leave this one in the 'no direct experience or compelling evidence as yet' category.

The dharma is about embracing the whole of our lives in service of full human flourishing - now. Whether there are heavenly realms, supernatural powers or beings, other lifetimes etc. etc. is not essential to the practice. Worse, it is distracting from what Gotama spent 45 years teaching.

These questions are not helpful in our bid to understand how to make peace with the inevitable difficulties of life and to release the habits of creating more of them. So I'd invite you to let them go through to the keeper[1] as you explore the dharma.

Is the dharma anti-pleasure?

No. Our body–minds are wired to pick and choose, to find pleasure enjoyable and pain not so much. If we truly had no preferences, we wouldn't be able to choose between getting out of bed and not. It's what we do with the experience of 'wanting' that makes the difference.

There is some irony in the fact that some of the orthodox approaches to the dharma scorn sensuality, even the sensual pleasures from eating ice-cream, a good hug, the smell of jasmine blooming. Automatically pushing these things away is itself a form of aversion - the very birthplace of much unpleasantness. Yet that's the attitude that some take towards

---

This is a sporting term from cricket, where the person batting doesn't even attempt to hit the ball because it was a poor quality throw.

these pleasant life experiences.

The first time I met a Buddhist monk in person I was spending a weekend at a rustic Buddhist retreat near Sydney. The venue, home to several younger monks, was presided over by a senior monk. I knew nothing about the monastic rules, so when I was introduced to the senior monk I greeted him as I would anyone - smiled, said hello and extended my hand to shake his. He shook my hand and welcomed me.

As we did this I noticed a startled look sweep across the face of the younger monk standing nearby. I was puzzled. Later, during a talk by the senior monk, he mentioned his greetings that day and how they went against monastic rules which forbade monks to touch women … hence the look of horror from the younger monk.

He'd decided in the moment that friendliness was more important than following that rule, and he felt that withdrawing from such a greeting would do more harm than participating in it. I was impressed by him (the novice monk who was looking dour obviously disagreed with this judgment call), but it seems that very rule had come to stand for a form of aversion.

The key factors here are how well we can bring mindfulness to our experience of pleasure, whether it's controlling us, and how we respond to not getting it. Are we mindfully experiencing pleasure, ensuring that it doesn't cause harm? Or are we controlled by it, reacting on autopilot and letting our hunger for more, more, more drive our experience regardless of the consequences?

Awakening is referred to as 'the highest happiness'. I guess this is why it's so important to recognise the glimpses we have of it (Third Great Task) so that we have a felt experience of this alternative type of happiness. Both pleasant and unpleasant experiences will be part of the path.

If you increasingly experience awakening, you might find your relationship to pleasures will change. Energy and joy remain, and you'll probably even experience pleasure more fully, more intensely, because you are paying better attention to it. However you won't be mindlessly letting it into the driver's seat of your life, hungrily steamrolling over anyone and anything that gets in its way.

Is the dharma anti-passion?

Passion is often referred to in the dharma as a problem. However it's important to understand what's meant by passion in this context. It's not energy, nor enthusiasm, nor enjoyment that's seen as problematic - we've already seen that pleasure isn't a problem. What's problematic is when these things trigger reactivity, when we mindlessly let them into the driver's seat without thought for the consequences.

In our modern world 'passion' is one of those words that's sometimes a euphemism. For example, emotionally reactive people are often described as 'passionate'. I remember a soccer coach I had who was described as passionate. Really, he was a highly extraverted narcissistic bully.

You often hear about passion as an essential ingredient in achievement. Achievement has become one of those unquestioned goods in our society. While it can definitely be good and can play an important role in flourishing, it seems that people are easily addicted to it in our modern lives. 'He's passionate about his work' can be a euphemism for 'He's addicted to achievement'.

Ironically, achievement is in fact more attainable with a clear, non-reactive mind. However we need to take a good look at the 'more is better' assumption with it. While it can be very enjoyable, healthy and beneficial, it can be a clinging-to-pleasure, whether that's the desperate drive for the admiration of our peers, a sense of status, or material gain. Wherever there's desperation, there's reactivity (clinging to pleasure or pushing away unpleasantness) which means, you guessed it - more unpleasantness.

Chapter 4: Buddhism

Is Buddhism a religion?

The short answer is probably something like this: it wasn't originally, but it was turned into one. Well, many actually. But you don't need to subscribe to a Buddhist religion to practise the dharma. Let me explain.

At a Buddhist conference I went to, an audience member asked a monk this question. His answer was, 'For tax purposes, yes'. One of the things I love about the dharma is how frequently you encounter a sense of humour in teachers.

When you ask this of someone well educated in philosophy or religion, you usually get an answer that goes something along the lines of, 'It depends on what you mean by "religion"'. That in itself would be an entire evening's dinner party topic in such company. So let's go to dictionary.com, the person-on-the-street's source of definitions, and answer the question that way.

But wait. Even before we get going, there's another hitch. It depends on what you mean by Buddhism because there really is no such thing as a single Buddhism. And the differences between approaches are in many cases much more fundamental than the differences between say the Catholic and Anglican approaches to Christianity. For example, some approaches teach rebirth as a fact of life and place it at the centre of their religious beliefs; other approaches (such as the secular approach) treat the issue of an afterlife as irrelevant.

It's tempting to sort the approaches to Buddhism into traditional/religious/orthodox and modern approaches, but that doesn't quite work. While many orthodox approaches will satisfy many of the criteria for a religion (such as Pure Land and Tibetan Buddhism) others won't tick too many boxes at all (e.g. Zen). This can be rather unsatisfying for a newcomer to the dharma who's trying to get their head around Buddhism.

So for the sake of simplicity, and acknowledging up front that this is only a broad brush, I'll answer the question by suggesting the approaches have two generic relationships to the dharma. The first relationship is belief based, covering those approaches that emphasise and require the practitioner to believe certain propositions about the world and experience in order to practise.

Let's call the second group the practice-based relationship, which covers approaches that treat the dharma, not as something to be believed and followed, but as something to be tried, tested and explored experientially. This table shows where some of the more commonly known approaches to the dharma would sit.

Table 1: Some common belief-based and practice-based Buddhisms

Belief-based relationship to dharma	Practice-based relationship to dharma
Tibetan Buddhism	Ch'an, Zen, Sŏn (referred to from here on simply as Zen)
Theravada	Insight Meditation based on the Buddha's teaching, not monastic traditions
Pure Land	Secular Buddhism
Most Buddhisms falling under the 'Mahayana' banner except Ch'an (China), Zen (Japan)/ Sŏn (Korea)	Engaged Buddhism

Bear in mind that this is just one way to segment the approaches. For example, another could be the extent to which they emphasise studying Gotama's original teachings in the Pali canon. If this were the issue you'd sort the list differently.

Let's look at definitions of religion from dictionary.com, along with a broad-brushed answer to the question of whether the belief-based and practice-based approaches satisfy each of them.

Table 2: In what ways Buddhisms are religions

Definition of religion	Belief based	Practice based
• a set of beliefs concerning the cause, nature and purpose of the universe, especially when considered as the superhuman creation of an agency or agencies, usually involving devotional or ritual observances, and often containing a moral code governing the conduct of human affairs	Yes	No
• a specific fundamental set of beliefs and practices, generally agreed upon by a number of persons or sects: *the Christian religion: the Buddhist religion*	Yes	To some extent; more so with practices than beliefs
• the body of persons adhering to a particular set of beliefs and practices: a world council of *religion.*	Yes	To some extent
• the life or state of a monk, nun, etc.: *to enter religion.*	Yes	No, except for Zen
• the practice of religious beliefs; ritual observation of faith.	Yes	No

You can see that even with this very simplistic analysis there's not a straight answer. For example the approaches with a belief-based relationship to the dharma would more than likely agree that the Four Noble Truths are the core beliefs that they share and would have a similar interpretation of them. They would believe in rebirth as if it were a fact of life.

However the practice-based approaches include Zen which adheres to the same interpretation of the Four Noble Truths as the belief-based approaches, yet it doesn't emphasise studying the dharma. The practice-based group includes the secular approach which does emphasise studying the dharma but has a different reading of the Four Noble Truths.

Another example is that Zen is an organised approach with many rituals and practices that are common to, and required of, its adherents. It has a monastic tradition and emphasises one's lineage of teaching, claiming that any certified teacher has a link back to Gotama himself. Insight Meditation, Secular Buddhism and Engaged Buddhism have no uniform rituals or practices, no monastic tradition and no talk of lineage.

As a final note on this dissection of approaches, bear in mind that there are also many things that the different approaches have in common, for example: the recognition of the impermanence, unreliability and instability of all things; that all things arise as the result of certain causes and conditions being present; and that there is no independent, consistent, enduring identity that forms the 'self' (even though some of them also believe that the self is re-born).

So the most accurate answer to the question of whether Buddhism is a religion is probably 'yes and no'. Yes, it has been turned into a religion by several cultures over time. And no, it was originally a way of understanding the human experience and flourishing in life, and this approach has survived and is increasingly being revived.

What are the different schools of Buddhism?

When starting to explore the dharma, I thought I'd have to subscribe to a 'school' of Buddhism which made me a bit nervous. My in-built crap detector often seems to clash with orthodoxies as they rarely encourage questioning. So I was very relieved to find that the traditional schools of Buddhism that I'd heard of were just one part of a long evolution of the dharma and there was no need to sign up for anything.

However the different Buddhisms can be very confusing and sometime even confronting if you encounter adherents who see their own approach as the only legitimate one.

So I'd like to share a helicopter overview of the evolution of the dharma so that you can see the different versions of Buddhism in context. Hopefully that will help you avoid the trap of believing that any one approach is the only 'true' or 'authentic' dharma.

Buddhism's four-phase evolution

Buddhism has evolved through four phases.

1. The first is the period of *Canonical* Buddhism, the 45 years of Gotama's teaching career.

2. The next very long period is the *Traditional* or *Historical* Buddhism extending right up to the mid-to-late 1800s. This is the period that saw the emergence of the various Asian adaptations of the dharma. Three different movements arose during this time; these are the 'schools' of Buddhism most people encounter:

    a. Theravada: the oldest of the three movements and is derived from a word that means 'teaching of the elders'. It emphasises scholarly endeavour focusing mostly on the Abidharma (not Gotama's actual teachings). It's a conservative and male-dominated movement that emphasises male monasticism and downplays lay dharma practice. It's practised mostly in Thailand, Cambodia, Burma, Sri Lanka and Laos, that is, South-East Asia.

    b. Mahayana: an umbrella group that includes approaches like Zen. Mahayana means 'great vehicle' which alludes to the claim that it has a more open-armed approach welcoming lay people, including women, although it's also steeped in cultures that are often male dominated. It's practised in many central north and east Asian countries.

    c. Vajrayana: broadly speaking, Vajrayana Buddhisms are a subset of the Mahayana movement. This school is also known as Tantric Buddhism (tantra is not just about sex). It's a development of the dharma emphasising the use of rituals, mantras, meditation and yoga (tantras) designed to tap into the subconscious. This includes the well-known Tibetan Buddhism.

3. *Modern* or *Revival* Buddhism: the period up until the latter half of the 20th century, which saw multi-faceted dharma practice being made accessible to all, with the scriptures available to lay people for the first time. It also de-emphasised ritual and folk lore.

4. *Global* Buddhism: the short period since the late 20th century where the internet and affordable travel have caused the different Buddhisms to discover and learn about each other.

This period is seeing the West begin to adapt the dharma to our own culture and time.

During Gotama's life he did his utmost to prevent his teaching from being turned into a religion. For example he refused to name a successor or to designate any fundamental doctrine. Individual practice was the way, according to him.

However, this didn't prevent humans from doing what we do, and within only a couple of centuries his teachings had been institutionalised and integrated with the socio–political fabric of the cultures in which they found themselves. This was the period of Traditional Buddhism, during which time the Zen tradition also claimed to have 'lineage' all the way back to Gotama via his disciple, Mahakassapa - so much for leaving no anointed successor. The majority of 'Buddhists' alive today now devote themselves to the out-workings of this period of Traditional Buddhism.

Winton Higgins, a Sydney-based Secular Buddhist teacher, notes that the effects of this phase included privileging monastic orders; institutions becoming more dogmatic, hierarchical and patriarchal; and relegating lay practitioners to the inferior role of donating money and goods in return for monastics performing rituals and teaching consolations and certitudes. Gotama himself was elevated to an object of worship rather than an inspiration for practice and living, and the living tradition was turned into a folkloric, metaphysical belief system rather than a set of enquiry questions to inform a living practice of Gotama's insights.

When people refer to different types of Buddhism, it's usually the Buddhisms from the Traditional era that they are speaking of. There are two important points to note here. First, these approaches are from only one phase of Buddhism (albeit a long one). While they are the types of Buddhism most commonly encountered, they do not represent the whole dharma-practising community.

Second, while the Mahayana and Vajrayana movements include many schools of Buddhism, both they and the Theravada school are al soaked through with various Asian cultures, which are superfluous to the teachings themselves. Importantly, they include some values that are at odds with more recent Western ones, including misogyny, paternalism and hierarchical, non-consultative decision making.

The next period, Modern or Revival Buddhism, began in Sri Lanka in response to the arrival of Christian (especially Protestant) missionaries.

Higgins writes:

> "Ironically, this movement emulated the Protestants in putting great emphasis on lay practice, piety and charitable works; criticising the pretensions of the monastics; and discarding the overlay of superstition and folk belief that had accumulated around popular religious observance. Modern Buddhism had a rationalistic temper, but under its auspices, lay people gained access to the suttas … in written form for the first time. One commentator has actually dubbed this kind of Buddhism 'Protestant Buddhism', and it represents a partial de-religification of the tradition. At least among the new Sri Lankan middle class, it was highly effective. In the process, the heritage of the Pali canon was revived and placed in the hands of lay people.
>
> Certain aspects of Traditional Buddhism remained, however. The monastic–lay relationship was re-jigged but remained important, and the idea of dharma transmission through teacher lineages still held sway. As with the culture of modernity as a whole, modern Buddhism espoused the idea of rational progress through fidelity to a 'right way', in relationship to which all alternatives were 'wrong'."

We are now in the newly spawned period of Global Buddhism where the many and varied 'flavours' of Buddhism are all rubbing shoulders and attending each other's retreats. Just as the dharma adapted helpfully to Asian cultures during the Traditional period, it is now just beginning to be adapted to Western cultures. The very new movement of Secular Buddhism is deliberate and open about this agenda.

Is there a sacred text?

The earliest written record of Gotama's teachings is the Pali canon (a canon is just a collection of books or scriptures). Pali is the ancient Indian language in which the dharma was first recorded. Gotama lived in a pre-literate society and his teachings weren't committed to writing until around 250 years after his death, most likely in Sri Lanka.

We don't know for sure what language Gotama spoke, probably a dialect called Mogadhan. Pali itself is an artificial language created for memorising or recording scriptures so that people of different dialects could understand them. It isn't actually a spoken language. In this way, it might be compared with medieval church Latin.

The Pali canon is vast. It consists of three sections, known as the *Tipitaka* (*Tripitaka* in Sanskrit, meaning three baskets, referring to the containers used for the palm leaves on which it was first written). It's important to know at least a little about it because one of these baskets, the Abhidhamma, does not contain records of Gotama's words at all.

The three baskets are:

- **The Suttas**

    These include 5,434 records of conversations Gotama had with people and talks he gave over the 45 years he spent teaching, as well as 15 book-length works ranging between about 9 and 500 modern pages.

- **The Vinaya**

    This is the list of rules that cover the conduct of monks and nuns who were in Gotama's community. These developed over time, often in response to practical situations that arose.

- **The Abhidhamma**

    This literally means 'higher teaching'. This section does not contain Gotama's direct teachings: it is a commentary authored by Buddhist monks, starting from around a century after Gotama died.

I'm not suggesting that because the Abhidhamma was created by people other than Gotama, it has no value, but I've often seen words presented as quotes from the Buddha, yet the source is listed as the Abhidhamma!

This basket was elevated to be part of the canon by monks in the Traditional Buddhist approach called the Theravada, who, like all of us, had their own agendas, lenses and world views. For that reason, it's important to distinguish this from the suttas.

Later Buddhist canonical texts are vast and diverse. In the millennia after Gotama died, the dharma spread orally in different languages throughout most of Asia. One of these evolved into Pali and another into Buddhist Hybrid Sanskrit. The Mahayana canon, of which there are many versions, dates back to around the 1ˢᵗ century CE and is broadly the canon followed in East Asian countries such as China, Japan and Korea.

The Tibetans also constructed their own in the 8th century CE. They translated Sanskrit texts including Mahayana Sutras and tantras as well as a scattering of material from Sanskrit versions of the Pali canon. In the 11th century CE they undertook a second wave of translations from Sanskrit, again including a wide range of materials.

Orthodox Buddhists may see the canon at the heart of their religion as a sacred text. While the secular approach to the dharma doesn't treat any text as sacred, it does emphasise the importance of studying the suttas from the Pali canon as a means of knowing for ourselves, as accurately as possible, what Gotama actually taught. That way the myriad Buddhist literature from later times and different cultures can be received through an informed lens.

Chapter 5: Dharma practice

My very first encounter with Buddhism was prior to the meditation retreat I told you about. A while before that I had seen a cute little flyer in the hairdresser's for 'drop-in classes' held a few suburbs away. My husband and I went along to find out about it.

That was almost the last thing I had to do with Gotama's teachings - it almost turned me off completely.

We entered and sat down with the dozen or so people in the small room. A few minutes later everyone stood up and in came a shaven-headed nun in robes. She proceeded to give a talk that was so un-enlightening (pardon the pun) and facile that Buddhism was almost thrown into the 'just another religion' basket there and then.

When I think about that experience, and how close I came to missing out on this deeply wise body of insight, I feel very grateful for the fact that it came around again in my life in a different form. I also feel for the many others out there who would love it but are turned off by their first encounter with what is probably a randomly chosen school of orthodox Buddhism.

Choosing an approach

The approach to the dharma that initially drew me in was Insight Meditation (IM), often referred to by its Pali name *vipassana*. IM is not a set practice or doctrine, rather it's a general term for practices that aim to develop insight.

Two well-known formulaic approaches within this school are the Goenka and Mahasi traditions from Burma. Goenka was born and trained in Burma and then returned to India (whence his family came) to teach IM. Goenka's process is a very tightly structured and strictly monitored approach to meditation and the dharma, most well-known for its standard 10-day retreat.

The Mahasi method also has its set practices (e.g. the practice of labelling or 'noting' experiences as they arise and pass away), however it's not structured as a program. These formulaic approaches are based on the Abhidhamma - the basket of the Pali canon that was developed by Buddhist monks well after Gotama's death.

I knew I would struggle with a rigid approach, so I was lucky to have access to a less formulaic version of IM as practised in Australia and other places around the world. This approach to IM doesn't have a special name, simply referring to itself as Insight Meditation. It's similar in attitude to secular dharma, although it doesn't pursue the goal of adapting the dharma to the current time and place and is more focused on insight than serenity, whereas secular dharma doesn't prioritise either.

Insight Meditation allowed me to explore the dharma in a self-directed way, drawing on practices and writings from other approaches and indeed all bodies of knowledge if they offered anything that I found helpful.

Importantly though, this was not a smorgasbord approach where you just pick whatever appeals to your taste. As with secular dharma, the IM teachers I was exposed to, based their teachings on the Pali canon. This ensures that what's chosen as 'helpful' is consistent with what Gotama taught, rather than some kind of feel-good spiritual consumerism. This approach seemed to be quite secular in its orientation while still allowing room for those who adopted some of the religious beliefs or practices.

It was in this spirit that I founded the Secular Buddhism Australia website, joining the existing movements in the US and the UK (and now in many more places around the world). Secular Buddhism is a very recent grass-roots movement which seems to be springing up across the Western world. As Stephen Batchelor once said to me, 'It's an idea whose time has come'.

As I see it, the task of adapting Gotama's teachings to our place and time, and sharing them in a way that speaks to us and our values, is not only an incredibly important project of compassion for others, but it' also a task that's entirely aligned with Gotama's own life. This approach makes dharma practice accessible and meaningful by bringing it into a working relationship with our own culture.

Some people find an orthodox school of Buddhism that they identify with that gives them a sense of belonging and which helps them learn and live the dharma. As long as it's achieving that outcome well, and not bolstering a sense of identity that they are clinging to and defending (more on that later), that's great. For those not moved to that path, Insight Meditation and secular dharma practice offer a rich alternative.

Do I need to go to an Asian country to learn the dharma?

I remember asking this question of Winton Higgins who was one of the regular teachers at my meditation group. His answer was a resounding 'No' and carried with it a caution that as a woman I'd probably find it pretty tough going if I did trot off to an Asian monastery.

Buddhism has been infused with the cultures it has encountered on its travels, many of which are paternalistic and misogynistic. Indeed one blogger I follow (Stephen Schettini), an ex-Tibetan monk writes:

> "Tibetan culture is deeply stratified. The Tibetan language itself has different vocabularies for speaking up to a superior, across to a peer or down to an inferior. The everyday name for woman is, 'low-born'."

A woman in my meditation group shared her own experience of spending several months in an Asian Buddhist monastery. She would watch dumbstruck as the deeply experienced adult nuns bowed and made way for the young boy-monks any time they were around.

Do I need to find a 'teacher'?

Yes. Lots of them. 😊

Two main forms of learning are involved in becoming a dharma practitioner. The first is to become familiar with the basic content of

Gotama's teachings. In this day and age vast amounts of information are available. Hopefully this book will help begin that type of learning.

The other type of learning is how to implement the teachings in your life. If you are lucky, there might be a dharmic meditation group near where you live. This type of group is often called a sangha which is the Pali and Sanskrit term for 'spiritual community'. This can be a highly effective way to integrate the dharma into your life as well as to give and receive encouragement and energy for the task.

However, even if you don't have access to a group there are many ways to teach yourself to live the dharma from journaling, online practice groups, attending Buddhist retreats, counselling by Buddhist psychotherapists, finding a dharma buddy for peer coaching, or simply using action learning techniques that harness self-reflection. At the time of writing, there is a donation-based online course in Secular Buddhism (search *Secular Buddhist Network*), and I also offer an online personal growth program based largely on the dharma (search *Flourish Personal Growth*).

When it comes to integrating the dharma into life, be mindful of the Buddhist saying that 'your enemies are your teachers'. This essentially means that whenever you encounter difficulty with another person, that's a little flag telling you that there's an opportunity for learning to practise the dharma. It's in that sense also that my answer to whether you need a teacher is 'Yes, lots of them'. These kinds of teachers, at least, aren't hard to find.

Some traditional schools of Buddhism emphasise hitching your star to an individual teacher as your guru in a master–apprentice type relationship. I've heard and read of this being beneficial and there are certainly times in my practice where individual access to a teacher has been helpful for me.

However it's not essential, and in some ways it's out of step with our culture and what we know of adult learning. As with all institutionalised hierarchies the guru–disciple relationship with its power imbalance predisposes itself to abuse, and like all religion Buddhism is not free from this. With so many podcasts, vodcasts, books, blogs, online courses and websites freely available now, with the many retreats and workshops on offer, and with the educated questioning minds at the helm of many groups, there really is no need for this kind of exclusive teacher–student relationship.

This is lucky as there aren't that many teachers to go around.

It's worth adding here, that it's not helpful to expect any one teacher to be a perfect exemplar of every aspect of the dharma. If we're only open to learning from teachers who are perfect, we're not going to learn much. Teachers are human too and they're walking the path and negotiating the challenges of their own messy humanness just like we are. As long as they are embodying some aspects of the teaching, learn from those aspects that are well developed and look to other sources to learn the things they can't teach you right now.

Some teachers might be great at helping you understand the concepts in the dharma, others might be good role models of open-heartedness and ego-lessness (not self), or of empathy, or of generosity. Others might inspire you with creative works – the power of beautifully crafted words or visual art to bring the dharma alive.

My own approach to teaching includes sharing my own struggles and dharma-failures and how I'm dealing with them. People tell me that this is in fact really helpful. Not all teachers are as willing to share their imperfections, but this is one advantage of the secular approach – we can learn from many sources, we don't need to hitch our star to any one person or source.

A secular approach

Every traditional approach to the dharma has been interpreted and integrated through at least one Asian cultural language and lens (sometimes more). It seems unhelpful to rely on, for example, the works based on the Tibetan cultural transmission of the ancient Sanskrit translation of the (probably) Mogadhan teachings (and other works) and translate them centuries later into English.

That's not to say we can't include this material in our practice – we may need different things at different times in the journey. But we don't want to rely on it as our North Star for what the Buddha taught.

With the knowledge we now have available to us in linguistics and philology (the study of ancient texts to determine their original form), it's far better to go as close to the source as we can, understand the message and then implement and communicate it in a way that makes sense to us in our Western lives. Once we're clear on the core teachings, we can make use of any and all works that resonate with us, knowing for ourselves how consistent they are with the teachings.

My experience also tells me that many of the views and values that have meshed with the traditional schools are indigestible to those of us in the West. Some of the views and values that came out of India with the dharma were not palatable to the Chinese, Koreans, Japanese, Burmese, Tibetan and Thai cultures for example, so they adapted the teachings to their own ways.

I believe the dharma will be most useful in the West if we see the wisdom in what traditional schools have done and adapt it to our own views and values, rather than adopting the previous foreign cultural adaptations. These values include the freedom to explore, question, challenge, compare, test and wrestle with a body of knowledge ourselves. They also include values of equality between men and women and consultative (rather than hierarchical) decision making.

Our modern education teaches us to think for ourselves, to be wary of swallowing whole the teachings of anyone else, and to decipher with logic, observation, reason and experimentation, what's helpful and what isn't. This attitude is entirely in keeping with Gotama's teachings and it's very useful to harnessing the power of the dharma.

Rather than recommend any approach I'll simply share the reasons that a secular approach appeals to me. This approach is more in line with the 'think, experiment and decipher for yourself' mentality than has been my (albeit limited) experience with other approaches.

At the same time it allows us to draw on anything that's helpful to our practice. We can draw from the orthodox approaches any practices, teachings, or inspirational creations that are helpful, as well as the ever-mounting body of thought and knowledge that Western culture generates.

The key point is to find and use whatever in the dharmic toolbox works for you. I'll say more about what I mean by 'works' soon, but a a quick summary:

- Whatever helps you see, expect and accept that unpleasantness is a part of life, and get to know fully the reality of your own experience (the pleasant and the unpleasant aspects of it, and all the bits in between).

- Whatever helps you let go of or dismantle your reactive habit of trying to make pleasant things last forever and unpleasant things disappear forever.

- Whatever helps you notice and become intimate with the state of non-reactivity and the wonderful lived experience that flows from this.

- Whatever is conducive to these three things and non-harm in the areas of:
    - your understanding of how your experience works
    - your thoughts and intentions
    - your speech and its impact on you and others
    - your actions generally (the extent to which they cause harm)
    - the way you earn a living or transact with the world
    - the amount of effort you make in pursuing these things
    - your awareness
    - the integration of your mental life (the extent to which it all drives in the same direction).

These points are a quick summary of what is traditionally called 'The Four Noble Truths' which we cover in detail in the next section.

I want to reiterate an important point about the secular dharma's openness to all sources. It's most definitely not an attitude of just picking and choosing whatever feels good or 'spiritual' or that moves us emotionally and deciding 'this works for me'. 'Whatever works' doesn't mean 'Whatever feels good'.

Dharma practice involves challenging and questioning ourselves, working to understand the teachings and implement them in our lives. These practices do lead to wonderful things, but they can be challenging and confronting and hard emotional work!

If we find ourselves choosing ideas and practices that simply justify or spiritualise our current opinions and attitudes; if we're simply adopting a new identity that we now protect and project into the world; if we aren't actively and honestly exploring and questioning our ways of looking at experience, thinking and behaving, then we're probably not practising the dharma.

How do I float my own boat?

With so much information and teaching available to us through podcasts, books and websites now, it's far easier to get ourselves onto the path than at any time in history. Finding a Buddhist meditation group and non-dogmatic Buddhist teachers will be a big help, but even if you don't, you can go a long way down the path on your own.

A famous story told by Gotama is that of the raft. He spoke of a man who was on a journey and came across a stream that he very much wanted to cross. There was no ferry, so he gathered together sticks, twigs, leaves, whatever would float, and cobbled together a raft. He then climbed on, put in a lot of effort with his hands and feet, and got to the other side.

The story warns people about getting too hung up on the means of achieving this way of life and losing sight of the fact that the means are simply in service of a goal. In essence Gotama was suggesting we gather together whatever floats our boat (or raft) and use it - whatever gets you there, whatever you have at your disposal that helps you with your undertakings. And once you've reached the other shore, you don't need to carry the raft around with you anymore.

These days the story might have had the traveller finding empty plastic bottles, bits of foam, some tyre tubes. In real life our raft might consist of books, CDs, podcasts, YouTube videos, websites, online courses, talks and practices by particular teachers that make sense or move us in the direction of the dharma (from any tradition of Buddhism or outside of Buddhism) or friends who have wisdom about these things, meditation retreats, meditation, yoga, poetry or other forms of art that help us experience the 'whatevers' from the list above in emotional ways. These days, we have available many, many items for creating our own boat to cross that stream.

To assess whether something really floats, ask yourself:

- Does this help me see, expect and accept all aspects of the human experience, the pleasant, the unpleasant and everything in between? Importantly, does it help me embrace the reality of unpleasantness in life?

    ◦ Hint: If it encourages you to ignore, deny, suppress, or denigrate any parts of the human experience, it probably doesn't float.

- Does this help me let go of or dismantle my reactive habits of desperately clinging to pleasant things and desperately trying to rid myself of unpleasant things? Does it help me see through the delusion that people and things 'out there' can make me indelibly happy? Does it help me truly integrate the impermanence of everything into my world view? Does it help me let go of a fixed idea about 'who I am'?

- Hint: Always trying to be happy, trying to force yourself into permanent states of bliss, and shutting out unpleasant experiences don't float well. If it encourages you to pin your happiness on any thing, person, practice or idea, it probably doesn't float. If it encourages you to reinforce a set identity, it probably doesn't float.

- Does this help me recognise and fully inhabit the experience of non-reactivity and its consequences – contentment, equanimity, energy, delight?

  - Hint: Getting addicted to blissful states or a new identity as a Buddhist is a form of reactivity.

- Does this help me understand clearly how my experience works, foster intentions, speech, action and a livelihood that lies somewhere between harmlessness and kindness? Does it help me cultivate spiritual effort (in sustainable amounts), mindfulness and/or a unity of mental activity?

  - Hint: If your practice is only something you do on a meditation cushion, your boat is probably not floating terribly well.

If the answer to any of these questions is no, the practice you're considering is unlikely to float your dharmic boat.

Three indispensable boat-construction materials

I want to share three construction materials that to me seem indispensable.

Meditation

The first is meditation. There are two reasons for this. First, from my own experience I know that in our busy modern lives, awareness of the many elements of our experience does not come naturally. Our minds and bodies are so busy moving that we rarely get to see the component parts of the movement experience.

Think of a puddle in a patch of dirt. If the water is moving, you can't see the bottom because the sediment is all stirred up, it's too murky. You need to let the pond settle in order to see its contours clearly.

Meditation is like letting the pond settle. We have so much stimulation in life today that the need for this is possibly even greater than in Gotama's time.

The second reason I see meditation as indispensable is that Gotama, despite being a fully awakened being, never stopped doing it. Indeed he once said, 'Practise like your hair's on fire'. He clearly saw it as an important part of floating your boat so that you make it to the shore.

Suttas in the Pali canon

The second indispensable boat-making material for those of us who don't come from a Buddhist background is becoming familiar with the core suttas from the Pali canon. This is how we can develop discernment about what floats and what doesn't, how we can differentiate between things that look like they float but either sink or bob just beneath the surface, and things that actually support us in our effort to reach the shore.

Even the earliest record of Gotama's words need to be seen in context - remember they weren't written down until a few hundred years after he died. However the method used by his followers to agree on and hand down the teachings is pretty respectable.

A few months after Gotama died, a big group of his followers came together for the First Council. Gotama's cousin, Ananda, recited as much of Gotama's teachings as he could. Ananda was Gotama's attendant and was at his side for the last 25 years of his teaching life. He also happened to have a memory like an elephant.

As Ananda recalled the teachings he'd state where they were at the time of the conversation, who was there and what was said. Others who had been at the relevant place and time would verify the story, and it was then accepted as a bona fide teaching.

Because India at the time was a pre-literate society the suttas were memorised by turning them into chants and reciting them frequently. Think about it, if you're reciting a chant as part of a chorus, you find out pretty quickly if your version has changed from the original and you fall back into line.

A few hundred years after his death, some monks and nuns transcribed the teachings onto palm leaves. It was now much easier to insert new teachings or interpretations. As the shelf life of palm leaves is short, they needed to be written and re-written frequently over time - plenty of opportunities for amendment.

It's only relatively recently that linguistic analysis of the style, tenor, grammar and syntax of the writings has deciphered what was likely the original teachings, and what was later added in.

While not a perfect transcript of what Gotama said, the suttas of the Pali canon are as close as we can get. Many scholarly writers have studied these scripts and identified where they might have been added to or tampered with after the fact. However in setting out to explore the dharma, this depth of analysis is not necessary as there are many good authors who have summarised core suttas.

It's also worth noting here that approaches like Zen don't emphasise knowledge of the suttas. I attended a Zen/Insight Meditation retreat once and was shocked to find that very few of the Zen practitioners were familiar with the teachings, relying instead on their teachers.

Zen emphasises experiencing the teachings rather than knowing them. So for example, Zen koans are riddle-like propositions designed to befuddle the rational mind, to get it out of the way so that you can experience the concepts rather than intellectually knowing them.

For me, of the traditional approaches I've encountered, Zen is the most accessible. However, in our modern societies I find that many people are unable to proceed down a path unless their thinking mind gives the green light - our crap detectors need to be calm – so we need to involve them. It usually takes time and dedication to know our experience clearly, and without the mind's green light, many won't stick with it long enough to achieve that clarity.

I've also found that bringing together the intellectual understanding with awareness, dedication to practice, and an openness to other approaches has been very powerful. That is why I consider knowledge of the core teachings from the Pali canon to be an essential boat-floating material in our modern societies.

Good friendship

The third essential boat-building material is to find yourself some good friends on the path. Gotama's cousin Ananda once commented that good friendship was half of the path. Gotama told him he was wrong - it's the whole of the path!

I've experienced the benefit of this. In 2009 I started a meditation group in my local area. For the first three years I was the only person with a key to open the hall each week. There were many weeks where I was so busy with life that it would get to Thursday afternoon and I'd find myself thinking, 'I could really do with a free evening tonight'. But because I was the only one with a key I had to go.

Every single time, without exception, when I was driving home afterwards, I thought to myself, 'I am SO glad I went tonight'. After three years, the value of regular attendance with my group of fellow travellers was so well entrenched that I didn't even think about not going. In fact I shared this experience with the group and offered the job of 'key holder' to anyone who'd like some help attending more regularly. I've rarely been the key holder since then. It's my weekly reset button, a vital and nourishing part of my life.

It's easy to find good friendship on the path if you have a local meditation group, but it can be a challenge if you live somewhere without enough like-minded people. Perhaps you can find it with a friend who's also interested in the dharma, or it might be with an online community. Attending a retreat is a great way to tap into these resources.

The myriad approaches to the dharma available these days can be both a blessing and a curse. It's a blessing in that we have access to many ways of implementing the dharma, those many bits and pieces that can help float our boats. However the down side of this is that it's easy to lose sight of the selection criteria for good boat-floating materials. In the two and a half millennia since Gotama lived, many written works claim to come from what 'the Buddha said', often with no reference whatsoever.

Many of the Buddhist works that have been created over the millennia could be useful for your practice, but the enquiring mind knows it needs a way of to anchor itself as it wades through the many resources on offer. We need to be able to decipher which are well aligned with the dharma and which might be infused with other agendas (e.g. making us feel good; getting 'likes'; selling to us; maintaining the status quo; cultural values such as deference to men in patriarchal societies, or the preservation of dharma practice being only available to monastics). The enquiring mind would know that it needs to account for the values and motives - the lenses of the authors, which are not always openly declared.

My hope for this book is that it too might be a helpful flotation device.

PART 2

THE FOUR GREAT TASKS

Chapter 6: The First Great Task

See, expect and accept unpleasantness

To recap, the orthodox version of the First Noble Truth is: the truth of suffering. The definition of suffering is:

- birth
- sickness
- old age
- death
- being parted from things we love
- being thrown together with things we don't like
- not getting what we want
- our whole vulnerable psycho–physical condition as humans.

That is, all of life is suffering.

Life is unpleasant?

This is one of the most common and gross mistranslations of this task. It's a damaging mistake because it turns people away. Here's an example, posted on a blog following an interview with Stephen Batchelor on Australia's ABC Radio National (20 Nov 2011):

> "Buddhism is anti-life. In his book An Open Heart, the Dalai Lama says over and over again things like 'the miserable nature of life' and that life is 'endless cycles of misery.' Buddhism says life sux, so kill off your life instincts and drop out; don't play the game.
>
> Buddhism says little about the positive things in life. It doesn't want to develop the full human being who can deal with life as it is. It is a teaching of resignation. It cops out and says there is no self anyway. But, there [sic] different selves beyond the ego personality. Buddhism doesn't teach you how to live as a complete human being."

The fact that life contains unpleasantness is very different from the assertion that all of life is unpleasant. It's also a more accurate reflection of Gotama's teachings. When you look at the sutta in the Pali canon where Gotama first articulates the Four Great Tasks, he says:

> "This is difficult space: birth is difficult space, ageing is difficult space, sickness is difficult space, death is difficult space, encountering what is not dear is difficult space, separation from what is dear is difficult space, not getting what one wants is difficult space. This psychological/physical condition is difficult space."

I've used the literal translation 'difficult space' here rather than unpleasantness because I find that it really works in this context of Gotama's original explanation of dukkha.

We know from our own experience that life has all sorts of things in it, some that would fall under the umbrella of unpleasantness or difficult space in our life, and many that don't (joy, compassion, love, fun, humour just to name a few). Indeed, when Gotama was directly asked whether all of life is unpleasantness, his response was essentially, 'If it was we wouldn't run about clinging to all the good stuff as we do'.

He stated that life was made up of three things: unpleasantness (dukkha), ease/happiness/pleasure (sukha) and quenching of the fire (nirvana) and declared that flourishing is the product of understanding and practising the Four Great Tasks.

The misinterpretation 'life is suffering' is likely to come from the last of the seven types of difficult space in the definition, the one that covers our entire psycho–physical condition. That is, our body-mind that has built into it these tendencies for fear and self-protection, for pain and disintegration, for reactivity. However they are not the whole of our experience. The *Five Clusters* of the human experience is one of Gotama's lists that helps us see this. But before we go there, let's look at what he believed the human experience was.

The human experience

In the Sabba sutta (the discourse on 'the all'), Gotama in addressing his followers, essentially says to them, 'Listen up, I'm going to tell you about everything that is'. He lists off six things: the five senses (and perception through them) as well as our mind and perception through this. He says, 'That's all there is and don't believe anyone who tells you otherwise. Anyone who tells you otherwise will run into trouble sooner or later because they won't be speaking from their own direct experience, and so won't be able to substantiate their claims'.

This is important. Gotama was clearly saying that our entire experience is made up of these six senses and our perception through them. That's all! We are literally sensitive beings whose entire experience is made up of contact between our six senses and various stimuli. He often referred to this as our *sensorium*. We are walking sensoriums (technically, sensoria).

So with that as the bottom line, let's get back to the Five Clusters (also sometimes called the five heaps, five aggregates, five bundles) as a way of paying attention to this 'all'. This is simply a way of grouping important aspects of our experience to help us observe it and see how it's always changing, depending on causes and conditions at the time. It's not meant to be a definitive, exhaustive list of every element of experience: it's a helpful way of scanning and paying attention in more detail than we ordinarily might.

Table 3: The Five Clusters

Cluster 1: Body Sensations

The five physiological senses we are used to (taste, physical sensation, smell, sound, sight) plus the mind. Gotama considered the mind to be a sense organ in that it receives and processes data that we then react to.

This cluster refers to the experiences that arise from our sensorium coming into contact with data.

Cluster 2: Feeling Tones

The general tone of pleasant, unpleasant or neutral, that emerges with every experience. Various 'feelings' or emotions we might experience (frustration, sadness, excitement etc.) all have a Feeling Tone.

Cluster 3: Perceptions

The way we recognise, name and label things in our world; the knowledge and concepts we use to identify the raw sensations.

You can feel your mind searching around to figure out what this image is: is it a silhouette of a face? Is it a bird? We want to attach it to a concept, a name. That's the process of perception in action - the attachment of concept and meaning to sensory data (in this case visual data).

Cluster 4: Reactions

Our reactions and responses. The thoughts and emotions that are habitually associated with these sensations and concepts - the 'stuff' that's associated with the experience, as well as our deliberate responses.

Reactions come up automatically from our body–mind as a result of the previous three heaps, for example memories, habitual thoughts, feelings, inclinations. It also includes our assumptions and paradigms, the narratives and the mental movies we allow to run in our minds, as well as our automatic reactions to these.

The pinball machine is reflective of the way something inside us is set off, and how coming into contact with different elements produces all sorts of effects: lights, noises, sometimes pleasant, sometimes not. Once the ball's been flung in our body, it requires awareness, intention, and skill to interrupt and de-power the pattern - to respond intentionally rather than automatically.

Cluster 5: Consciousness

The conscious awareness of any of the above and the mind activity we create and allow in response to that awareness. I say 'create and allow' because some mind activity is consciously conjured up, that is, we know we're asking our mind to pay attention to something or answer a question or think something through.

However, minds think most of the time. That's what they do, in the same way that eyes see all the time and ears hear all the time. So even when we're not deliberately harnessing our thinking power, it hums away in the background. It's constantly naming and reasoning and describing and hypothesising about things because it's had a lifetime in the role of protector. Consciousness also includes this unbidden conscious mind activity that we allow to continue once we realise it's there.

I chose this picture to remind you of what's in focus, and the fact that, by paying attention, we can to a large extent determine that focus. Our Consciousness can dictate what we pay attention to (if you've never seen the Invisible Gorilla clip on YouTube, search for it; it's a great example of this) and it's Consciousness that allows us to make intentional choices about responding rather than reacting on autopilot.

Here's an example from a session with my meditation group to bring the Five Clusters alive:

- Sensations: Sound waves hit my ear drums.

- Feeling Tone: I experience pleasure; I like it!

- Perceptions: I recognise the sound as rain on the roof of the deck under which we're meditating. I recognise the sound as rain falling on a tin roof.

- Reactions: I imagine being tucked up, warm, inside at home on a cold rainy day, as well as memories of summer storms in Brisbane. Memories of mangoes and frangipani flowers arise. There's a sense of the rain closing us in together: a sense of togetherness, safety, enjoyment of nature.

- Consciousness: I'm aware that a smile has crept across my face. As the rain gets heavier I'm aware that the smile grows bigger. I'm aware of the positive Feeling Tone and the enjoyment of being here with others. I think about the need for connection and how this is being filled at the moment. I'm aware of my love for nature. I imagine telling the group about my involuntary smile when the meditation is over.

If you interpret Gotama's words as meaning the seven types of difficult space are nothing but pain, then you can see how it could be logically deduced that all of life is unpleasant. The Five Clusters pretty much cover the entire human experience, so if they are the definition of unpleasantness, then yep, 'life sux'.

However, we know he didn't teach this because when he was asked directly, he expressly said life contained unpleasantness, ease and quenching of the fires. He was saying that, among other things (such as ease and quenching), all clusters of the human experience can contain unpleasantness – the seeds are there for it. Life involves unpleasantness, not life IS unpleasantness – it's an integral part of the package, not the whole package. In this light it makes sense that:

- Sensory stimuli can be painful (fingernails scraping down a blackboard, anyone?).

- We can have a strong negative Feeling Tone about something (maggots with your fruit?).

- We can have painful concepts or Perceptions about things (e.g. concluding that all of life is suffering).

- We can have painful memories or associations with things (e.g. the upset that might arise automatically when someone yells angrily).

- We can have pain from what we attend to (e.g. ruminating on mental movies about someone trying to undermine us).

Even pleasure is unpleasant?

Another common out-of-whack perspective is that because all things are impermanent, even joyful experiences are unpleasant … because they end.

If we have an expectation or desire that the pleasant things in life can be arranged to continue permanently, we are going to be disappointed. Most of us do secretly hold this wish, so we do often experience this disappointment.

However that doesn't make all worldly joys unpleasant. If we can enjoy something truly knowing, expecting, and accepting that it's temporary, its end doesn't have to be unpleasant.

I remember celebrating a friend's 40th birthday on his father's sailing boat. In the afternoon it rained for a couple of hours. A little while later three beautiful rainbows appeared in the sky. We sat there enjoying them, feeling very lucky to behold the scene.

Of course a short time later they faded and disappeared. There was no unpleasantness, as I fully expected them to fade; if anything there was a little afterglow of gratitude that we'd been graced with their presence. So if we can truly accept the temporary, impermanent, unreliable nature of all pleasures, they don't necessarily have to produce unpleasantness when they end.

If we look back over our own lives we know instantly that it's true - life contains difficult spaces. There is a natural unpleasantness (of varying intensities) that comes along with birth, sickness, old age, death, not getting what we want, getting what we don't want, being parted from things we love, and our whole psycho–physical condition. Our lives have contained many varieties of this stuff.

However very few experiences are all bad all the time. Along with the pain of childbirth comes the joy of a new baby. A friend of mine even describes childbirth as ecstatic (she's been through it twice). Along with sickness often comes a greater appreciation of health and the simple daily things. Along with old age can come wisdom and peacefulness. For some people death even brings relief.

The saying 'be careful what you wish for' acknowledges the fact that 'getting what we want' isn't always the joyous vision of happiness we expected it to be. As Oscar Wilde said, 'There are only two tragedies in life. One is not getting what you want, the other is getting it'. I'm sure we've all known the experience of wishing for something and not getting it, only to find later that we're really glad we didn't get it.

I had a vivid experience of getting what I wanted only to find it wasn't all beer and skittles. I'm a Masters athlete in track and field. In 2016 I came home from the World Masters Athletics Championships with no less than eight medals. This is pretty out-there, I couldn't have asked for anything better. Most athletes are over the moon if they manage to earn one!

And yet I noticed a subtle sense of disappointment in the following weeks. It hadn't really changed my life in any way. I realised I had an unspoken expectation that it would. It gave me some deep-seated confidence as an athlete, but other than that life just went back to normal.

As time went on I also noticed some unpleasant consequences: I now became the person everyone wanted to beat; every time I ran, expectations were high, so even really good performances were often seen as ordinary; and all of a sudden everyone seemed to think they had the right to an opinion about me – what I was doing right and wrong – I seemed to become public property somehow. I also found that people I didn't know started saying hello to me in passing, using my name, but I didn't know who they were, so I couldn't use theirs in return. It felt like I was being unfriendly.

There's very little in life that's all good or all bad.

So clearly, the idea that all of life is unpleasantness is no more accurate than the idea that all of life is pleasure. I've sometimes wondered why Gotama didn't formulate this insight as 'There's unpleasantness and joy' because that's clearly true. Or even 'Life contains all sorts of things, pleasant, unpleasant and everything in between'.

However, when I think about what he was trying to do, it makes sense. He was trying to show the way to peace and freedom by relaxing with the unpleasantness that's inevitable, letting go of our habit of creating a whole bunch more, and acquainting ourselves fully with the rich and wonderful experience that follows.

Given that as human beings we have a habit of desperately chasing the pleasant and running from the unpleasant, and given that this path requires us to drop that habit, he needed to focus us squarely on our relationship with unpleasantness. That's the linchpin to the paradigm shift that's required.

The Task: See, expect and accept unpleasantness

(SEA unpleasantness)

So what's the practical imperative of the reality that life contains unpleasantness? It is to see when and how it happens, to fully know the experience, to expect it in our life, and accept that it's part of being a human. Stephen Batchelor summarises this as 'embrace dukkha'. If we can do this, we stop fearing it so much. We stop carrying on about it. This reduces the amount of unpleasantness in our life dramatically.

Think about the springboard divers at the Olympics. Each of them hurls themselves into the air, does their acrobatic thing and then enters the water. The way they enter the water has a big impact on the score they are given. Those who enter with a big splash get lower scores, and those who enter it with only a small disruption to the surface get higher scores.

In a way, our mind is like the surface of that water. If we can accomplish the great tasks described in this book, unpleasantness enters our world like a high-scoring diver. Our body–mind registers that unpleasantness has entered the pool, but there's no splash and spray.

Some traditional approaches to the dharma claim that all unpleasantness can be eradicated, even physical pain, claiming that the perception of pain is simply a judgment of unpleasantness that the mind has been conditioned to make. The belief is that if you can change that perception, then voilà you're dukkha-free! No difficult spaces!

To me this doesn't add up. Babies feel pain as unpleasant, animals feel pain as unpleasant, and neither of them has cerebral judgments getting in the way. I can't help seeing this belief as part of a 'spiritual bypass' where we hope that being spiritual will somehow get us out of being human. Accepting and embracing the reality that unpleasantness is part of the human package brings us face to face with the truth of the human experience. Treating it as simply a miswiring of perception that we need to transcend appears to me like aversion.

The path that's more coherent with real life experience is to embrace the whole of this human-ness thing, unpleasant bits included, and to let go of the self-created helpings of difficulty. The goal is to stop the splash and spray, our reactivity to unpleasantness, and let this path lead us to travelling life with greater peace - to flourishing.

See unpleasantness

First of all we have to see the difficult spaces. If we can't see them in our lives then we're hardly going to get to know them, expect them in our day-to-day life, nor accept them. Of course some forms of unpleasantness are obvious such as the loss of anything that's cherished - loved ones, physical capability, friendship, belonging, freedoms, treasured possessions, money, even ideas about ourselves, others or the world. It also includes physical pain and sickness as Gotama identified.

However much of the unpleasantness that we experience on a day-to-day basis is not so obvious. This is where mindfulness comes in, both in the form of meditation and mindfulness in the everyday cut and thrust of life. As we practise mindfulness in our lives, we start to see that many of the experiences we've been choosing are actually unpleasant!

Let's look at some more experiences that might surprise you when you assess whether they are unpleasant or not. Each one describes a decision to do something you think is beneficial to you, but if you look closer it might be a variety of unpleasantness.

Pick a real situation in your own life that corresponds with one of these themes and look at it closely using the clusters:

- You describe one of your recent successes to a friend with whom you feel competitive.

- You bad-mouth someone to someone else.

- You cheat in a game or test in order to succeed.

- You express your opinion aggressively to someone who disagrees with you.

- You agree to do something you don't really want to do in the hope they will like you more.

- You tell a 'little white lie' to someone in order to get something you want.

- You insist that someone follows the rules even though it would have helped them and harmed no-one to bend them.

- You avoid talking to a close friend about an issue that's coming between you.

One tip for seeing unpleasantness is to increase your awareness of your body. In fact in using the word 'see', I really mean know it, attend to the experience of it, become intimately familiar with it.

I realised in my early thirties that I was out of touch with my own body. I pretty much lived from the neck up. However our bodies are very reliable indicators of whether something's 'going on' emotionally and whether that something is pleasant, unpleasant or neutral. They are very good messengers and we need to inhabit them and listen to them.

We know that unpleasantness is part of being human, so when we find some, it isn't necessarily a problem. The problem arises when we make a mess by what we do next, with the way we respond to it. I'll say a lot more about that with the Second Great Task, but for now, what we want to do is see the process we engage in once we've registered an unpleasant Feeling Tone.

For example, if I notice some tension or distance with a friend, do I just start avoiding them? Or do I ignore it and pretend I don't notice it? Neither of these reactions is great for the friendship, but the idea of talking about it feels stressful, that is, unpleasant, and I don't want to feel that. What if I've done something to upset them? I don't want to hear that!

Using the Five Clusters to inspect an unpleasant experience can help us see the processes that are bringing it about - the mental and emotional reactions that arise automatically, the habitual reactive choices we make when we feel unpleasantness (e.g. avoidance), and the conscious mind activity that follows. That mind activity might be a negative narrative about my friend, a justification for me not dealing with it, or imagined mental movies of having a big argument.

As we see the patterns more and more clearly, it registers just how temporary, fluid and ever changing these experiences are, how dependent on conditions they are, and we begin to get less fussed about them. Things not going smoothly with our friend isn't a big deal. It's a normal part of human relationship. So we might ask what's up. That alone shows care for our friend and we might even discover that they appreciate being able to share what's bothering them - which may or may not have anything to do with me!

Practical tip

A practical method I use for seeing, knowing, and embracing unpleasantness in the moment, is to do a scan across three parts of my experience:

1. **Mind activity:** What's there? Are there mental movies of imaginary scenarios showing at my internal cinema? Verbal narratives or responses perhaps? Am I building a case against someone? I try to simply describe what's going on in my mind as if I had to summarise it for someone else.

2. **Emotions:** What feelings are present? I try to put my finger on them. If I find myself listing words that are not really feelings, I try to get to the underlying feeling, e.g. I'm feeling betrayed. Betrayal is an interpretation of events, not a feeling. What's under it? Is it hurt? Fear? Embarrassment? Am I feeling afraid? Disconnected? Lonely? Sad perhaps?

3. **Body sensations:** Where do I feel these feelings in my body? How would I describe the feelings? Is there warmth? Movement? Shape?

So the first letter (S) in my little memory aid (SEA unpleasantness - **S**ee it, **E**xpect it, **A**ccept it) for the First Great Task uses the word 'see' to mean really get to know it. Grow your awareness of where unpleasantness arises in your life and get curious about it, so that you know it well, how it works, the mechanics of it, and how it shows up for you in the body, mind and emotions.

Expect unpleasantness

If you were to create a poster for a movie called 'My Future', what would be on it? If you have the time and some coloured pencils or crayons around, maybe have a go at doing this before you read on.

For many people this poster will contain lots of pleasant things. There might be career progress, wealth or at least financial security, relaxation, travel, indulgence in hobbies, a loving relationship, some loving children or grandchildren, maybe some achievements or expensive toys as evidence of achievements, maybe awards and prizes, maybe fame of some kind. Most likely you've got all your body parts in this poster and you'll be there at a ripe old age, healthy and happy.

For others perhaps, the poster might be doom and gloom. It might be full of difficulty, ailments, loneliness and struggle.

Now do this activity. Take an A4 page, turn it sideways and rule a horizontal line across the middle. Then draw a marker on the line to represent each decade of your life to date, so that the page from left to right is a timeline of your life with markers to show each 10 year period. Now think about your life, decade by decade, and plot it as a graph. Above the line is pleasant (the further above the line, the more pleasant), below the line is unpleasant (the further below the line, the more unpleasant), and the middle horizontal line is neutral.

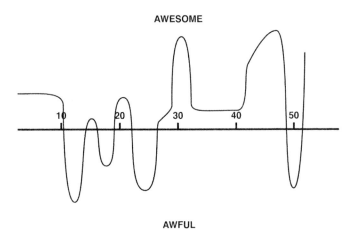

Chances are there are patches of your graph that are below the line and patches that are above it. Maybe they're just short spikes down into the lower half of the page or maybe they're long dips. But you'll be able to see quite clearly from your chart that life contains both pleasant and unpleasant things.

Now why is it that, based on our track record, we know life contains both pleasant and unpleasant things, but we hope or expect that our future won't? If your poster for the future movie is filled with highlights, take notice of the fact that in all likelihood the pattern will be up and down just like the rest of life.

If your movie poster is doom and gloom, take notice of the fact that real life has taken you both above and below the line. If it's never taken you above the line, then the most compassionate thing you can do for yourself is to seek some professional support. If it's never taken you below the line, you are one very lucky human being. Bear in mind that this is very rare and it will probably change.

If we have all-good movie posters, are we really expecting the full range of experiences in our future? When unpleasantness arises, are we knocked off course? Why me? This wasn't part of the plan! There's shock that cancer or the death of a loved one, or loss of a job, or failure of a business, or inability to reach a long-held goal, actually happened. We know this kind of thing happens, but we don't truly expect it to happen 'to me'. Shock at unpleasantness arising reveals an instance of us not really expecting it as part of life.

If we have negative movie posters, we might need to adjust our expectations in the other direction. Life contains pleasant things too. In fact studies looking at the ratio of positive to negative events in daily life show that there are typically many more positive 'events' in a given day than negative ones. So the task on offer for you might be to start noticing the daily experiences that have a pleasant Feeling Tone. (Rick Hanson's book *Taking in The Good* might be helpful for you.)

Cultivating a pessimistic view of the world is, in its own perverse way, an aversion. Often the rationale is that if I lower my expectations of life, then I'll never be disappointed. So I spend 99% of my time feeling unhappy in order to avoid the 1% of the time where I could experience the unpleasantness of disappointment.

It might also be that being 'down' garners support and encouragement from others, an attempt to fill the need for connection. However it's worth looking at this closely too. How long do people stick around when you act like Marvin the Robot? (Marvin was an insanely intelligent but depressed robot in *The Hitchhiker's Guide to the Galaxy* series.)

A large part of my career has been spent facilitating groups either in meetings or in various learning environments. One of the things I learned early on when managing a group was to make a plan and then to let the plan go. Things often don't go according to plan, so we need to hold it lightly and trust our ability to deal with whatever arises.

This plays out acutely for athletes. In 2018 I was the World Champion in the 400 m hurdles in my age group. I was on track to defend my world title and possibly even break the World Record, when in the final three months before the World Championships, I got an injury. I managed that and recovered in time, and then promptly contracted a virus that wiped me out. All I managed was a bronze medal.

To give you an idea of how much went into this goal, training at the elite level involves training six days a week, taking care with my food and sleep, planning any trips away around the location of athletics tracks, regular physio and massage and a good chunk of most weekends through summer spent at competitions. That's to say nothing of the pain involved in training for the 400 m! After three years of dedicated effort, having the rug pulled out from under me taught me to hold my goals lightly!

The same is true for the plans we have about our future. By all means do what you can to bring about the kind of future you want, but can you, at the same time, hold those plans lightly, knowing that you don't control everything that happens to you? Can you leave enough space on the movie poster for the unknown doses of unpleasantness that will definitely arise in your life? Can you perhaps just design the poster in pencil, to allow for amendments?

Practical tip

Identify or create something to remind you to hold your plans and expectations lightly - something that reminds you that your own intentions and actions are a part of the picture but only one part. It might be some version of the life-line you created earlier, an image, a song, a YouTube video, a written piece - anything that helps shift your expectations of life to be more aligned with the reality that life contains all sorts of things.

So the second letter (E) in my little memory aid (SEA unpleasantness - **S**ee it, **E**xpect it, **A**ccept it) for the First Great Task represents the challenge to expect unpleasantness in our life. Because we know it's a part of life, when we think about our future, or about something unpleasant happening right now, we're not shocked or surprised. Unpleasantness is a member of the household, not some foreign, unexpected, intrusive blow-in.

Accept unpleasantness

Accepting unpleasantness doesn't mean we sit on our hands if there's something we can do to remove pain from our lives. It's not about becoming a Buddhist doormat. What it means is that we first accept and are present to the situation. Then we respond from the place of acceptance rather than resisting the reality of what's happened and reacting on automatic pilot. Accept and respond rather than resist and react. The Star Trekkies out there will remember the Borg who insisted that 'resistance is futile'. Actually, it's worse. Resistance is unpleasant!

Examples: accept and respond vs resist and react

I remember a striking example of the pain of resistance. My husband Matt, my dog and I had just spent a month in Cairns in northern Australia. I love Cairns and would ideally live there for half of the year.

We were driving in two separate cars to a town four hours away. The next day, Matt would set off back to Sydney with our van and our dog and I'd return to Cairns to finish this book. It was the start of the end of the trip together.

The Feeling Tone as I was driving behind our van containing Matt and Taz, was unpleasant. I felt sad at the impending separation from them (separation from things we love), and a sense of being dragged against my will from a place I love, back into a crazy, crowded city. I actually love where I live in Sydney, but whenever I spend time outside of cities, I never want to plunge back into them.

For the first two hours as I followed Matt along the highway, I was battered around by a barrage of negative thoughts - what I call a negative eddy (like the eddy in the toilet). The mind activity was mostly mental movies and they were ridiculous.

First there were the driving movies which ranged from Matt and Taz having a horrible crash and being sprawled across the highway dead, to an out-of-control driver swerving onto my side of the road, me swerving to miss him, only to be hit head on by the next driver on the road.

Then there was the movie about me getting cancer and being on my death bed regretting having put off writing my book. And then there was the one about our business failing and us not having enough money for me to continue working part time which means I'd have to give up athletics and have no time for my dharma projects. My negative eddy was spiralling down further and further into the toilet.

This negative eddy was the result of my unwillingness to accept my circumstances. When there's an unpleasant Feeling Tone present, the mind goes looking for explanations, for causes - a self-protection mechanism. If it doesn't find any obvious or interesting causes, it starts making stuff up.

In my mind I was still actively wishing we could avoid going back to Sydney and could live in Cairns (resistance). I was putting mental energy into comparing the way life is at the moment with the way I wanted it to be, rather than accepting that Matt had decided to go home now and that we'd agreed we wouldn't consider living in Cairns for another few years. This non-acceptance was creating unhappiness and the unhappiness was creating the negative eddy.

About halfway through the four-hour drive, I brought some mindfulness to my situation and realised what was going on. I made a conscious decision to accept that we were going back to Sydney and staying there for the next few years.

What does it mean to 'accept' this? It meant I stopped playing the trailer for the movie called 'Living in Cairns'. It meant I stopped comparing the Cairns movie to the Sydney movie. It meant I stopped thinking about the lovely warm winter breezes, the chilled pace of life and the house we could buy in Cairns and be mortgage free. I took those movie trailers out of the mental DVD player and tossed them away.

The change in my state of mind was swift and pleasant. My body relaxed, the tension disappeared, and my mind was able to roam to other pastures. The sadness of being separated from Matt and Taz was still there when I thought about them leaving, but it was much less intense and intrusive than before.

In an episode of Star Trek, Data the android described missing someone: 'As I experience certain sensory input patterns, my mental pathways become accustomed to them. The inputs eventually are anticipated and even missed when absent'. That's a factual way of describing what it means to miss someone. When I could see that for what it was, the feeling of sadness at missing them was still there to an extent, but I was happier, calmer and so much freer. You can feel more than one thing at the same time.

My first international athletics competition was another striking example of the power of acceptance. I hadn't intended to go as I'd only been doing athletics for three years and didn't think I was good enough to be competitive. But six months earlier I had taken up sprint hurdles and as it turned out, I have a bit of a knack for them.

My hurdles coach was strongly encouraging me to go, telling me I could even 'medal'. I wasn't sure about it, but finally decided to go, as much for the experience of indoor racing (which I'd never had before) as for the competition. We did a time trial of the 60 m hurdles the week before we left and I did it in 9.5 seconds. Things were looking good.

The big unknown was how I would cope with having other hurdlers next to me. The truth is, even when I did hurdles as a youth I was always in front by the first hurdle so I had nothing to distract me. I'd competed at the Australian National Championships a few weeks earlier where the same was true. I was concerned that with faster hurdlers around me I might get distracted having them in my field of vision. Getting distracted in a hurdles race spells disaster.

I'd asked my coach if we could emulate race conditions somehow - maybe have someone sprint next to me while I do the hurdles. But he didn't take my concern seriously.

So the moment comes. I've travelled all the way to Budapest in Hungary and it's the day of my hurdles heat. We're called out to the race lanes in the middle of the indoor stadium. I'm excited, nervous and quite pumped about getting out there and doing it.

The gun goes off. At the first hurdle I'm equal first. I can see another hurdler off to my left. The novelty of this distracts me, I lose my concentration and with it, my forward momentum. Soon there are multiple people in my field of vision and they were passing me!

It was a terrible run of 10.28. Disappointment arose. 'Never mind', I think to myself, 'I'll do better in the final'.

However ten minutes later we discovered that the qualifying time for the final was 10.25. I'd travelled to the other side of the world for a race and missed out on it by 0.03 of a second!

As my coach and I sat together and looked at the qualifying time, I was first hit by a numbness, shock and disbelief. Then came crushing disappointment. Tears came up unbidden.

At this point I was in what I call 'the shift'. With loss of something valuable comes a shift in the landscape of your world: it's like the tectonic plates of the earth just moved. Sometimes they're small shifts like this one, and sometimes they're big shifts, like when you lose a loved one. The ground beneath you - the landscape you had accepted as solid, permanent, stable, or reliable - suddenly moves and reveals its impermanence. I find that tears come up automatically when I'm in the shift.

I don't know for sure but I suspect someone who's well practised at awakening may not get tears in the shift because they'd have truly adjusted their view of everything to be consistent with the nature of reality: impermanent, unreliable and unstable.

When one of Gotama's brightest and most intimate disciples died, we don't know what he felt, but the sutta describes no tears or mourning. Apparently he commented that a great light had gone from the world. Perhaps he felt sad, but my guess is that he wouldn't have experienced the shift. For the rest of us however, tears in the shift are a good indicator that we've lulled ourselves into believing that something dynamic and unreliable was fixed and a sure thing.

Next in my hurdles disaster story came the comparison phase of my mental movie - comparing the movie of what was 'supposed to happen' with what had just happened. Hanging on to what's supposed to happen is resistance: hanging on to it, replaying it, allowing it airtime in our mental cinema.

What I did next was strikingly helpful. I regained my composure then walked to the other side of the stadium where there were no people. I then let my body do what it needed to do - let out the grief.

One theory on why we cry is that it releases stress hormones after a stressful event. Research has shown that the chemical composition of upset tears is different to that of joyful tears or functional tears (e.g. those that remove something from your eye). Tears of upset contain greater concentrations of stress hormones such as cortisol. (From this perspective the expectation that men don't cry is quite cruel.)

Researchers mightn't be sure about the function of tears but as I sat alone on the steps with my head in my hands and tears flowing, it certainly felt like stress relief. I stayed there until I felt that I'd really let it all out and there was a sense of calm.

Next, I stopped thinking about what was supposed to happen and re-wrote my mental movie about the rest of my trip. I accepted what had happened and let the 'What's Supposed to Happen' movie dissolve. This is wise use of attention.

The result was that I really enjoyed the rest of my time in Europe. Indeed a couple of my fellow athletes remarked how surprised they were at my calmness and happiness in the face of such a colossal disappointment.

As an end note to the story, I knew I'd done a good job of acceptance when I saw the winning times and discovered that my 9.5 seconds would have won me a silver medal. There was no upset, no 'If Only' or 'Poor Me' mental movies, with me standing on the podium receiving a medal. In fact there was a little pleasure in the fact that I knew my time would have been competitive. Then the mind moved on.

My hurdles scenario is one where I had no choice about what happened. I couldn't change it or do anything about the situation itself. But how does acceptance work in a situation where you can actually change the outcome? Does acceptance mean not doing anything about it?

No. It means first accept that what's happened has happened. Ditch the What's Supposed to Happen movie and respond creatively.

This is the thing about non-acceptance and the reactivity that comes with it. They rob us of our full range of creative abilities. We get stuck in a rut, unable to see other possibilities because the mind is taken up with re-runs of mental movie comparisons and the body is flooded with stress and tension. When you put away the What's Supposed to Happen DVD, all of a sudden you have attentional bandwidth to create options, get perspective, and respond in a way that's helpful to yourself and others.

Practical Tip

When a situation doesn't go your way, take notice of the mental movies playing over and over at your internal cinema, especially those that involve comparison of what's happened with what was 'supposed to happen'. See if you can take those mental DVDs out of the player. Then take some time to acknowledge whatever disappointment or upset that's present and articulate to yourself what exactly it is that you're upset about - what is it exactly that you're upset is not arriving in your life right now?

When you've done that fully, ask yourself the question: with this as the situation, what's the most helpful thing I can do for myself or others, right now?

The final letter (A) in my little memory aid (SEA unpleasantness - See it, Expect it, Accept it) for the First Great Task represents the challenge to accept and respond to the situation rather than resist and react to it. It's the challenge to put away the "If Only" mental movies, the "What Was Supposed to Happen" mental movies, and any 'shoulds' or 'oughts', see the starting position in this moment as what's actually happened, and respond creatively. That is, respond in a way that's most helpful and kind for ourselves and others given what's happened has happened.

Summary

- The First Great Task is to incorporate the existence of unpleasantness into our view of normal life.

- Unpleasantness can be found in all sorts of experiences, even some that we initially think are going to bring us something pleasant. An important part of truly embracing unpleasantness is seeing it when it arises, even in surprising places.

- Very little in life is all good or all bad. Incorporating this fact into our ideas about what we want and don't want, what we think will make us happy and unhappy, can help us roll with reality more easily.

- We need to truly accept that unpleasantness is a normal, natural, inevitable part of life. It's part of the package of being human, not the only part, but an integral part. It's a member of the family, not an intruder.

- When we truly accept this, we incorporate it into our expectations of life, of our future. Just like the past, the future will involve all sorts of experiences, pleasant, unpleasant and everything in-between. We adjust our expectations to be more realistic.

- Accepting unpleasantness doesn't mean doing nothing when we can prevent unpleasant things from happening. It means accepting that what's happened has happened, and responding creatively in line with our values, rather than resisting reality and reacting mindlessly.

Chapter 7: The Second Great Task
Dismantle reactivity

The challenge with the Second Great Task is to dismantle the hungering habit that triggers reactivity - to let it go.

It's simple, but not easy.

With unpleasantness arises a hunger for things to be different. This hunger is often referred to as *craving*. Literally, the Pali word means *thirst*. I find hunger more relatable because you can be aware of a slight hunger or a strong hunger or something in between. We don't often feel strong thirst these days, so I find the range of hunger feelings more helpful. Any of these three is a perfectly good translation though.

When we feel this hunger, we react. Rather than accepting what has happened and then responding from a creative place, we waste energy resisting reality and reacting to the unpleasantness of it. There's some overlap with the First Great Task here but don't get hung up on that. I think of the Second Great Task as 'how to' truly embrace unpleasantness.

The problem is that we're not willing to simply allow the unpleasant experience, even knowing that it will come and go like everything else. Instead we react by trying to arrange things so that the pleasant stuff lasts and we avoid unpleasant things at all costs. We fan the flames rather than let them extinguish themselves, which they naturally do if we don't react.

Let's use the Five Clusters to see this reactive process we engage in when we experience unpleasantness:

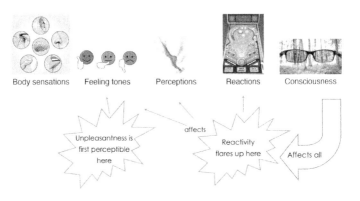

Body sensations   Feeling tones   Perceptions   Reactions   Consciousness

affects

Unpleasantness is first perceptible here

Reactivity flares up here

Affects all

Figure 1: The Five Clusters at a glance

Most of the time we're on automatic pilot. That is, we're not bringing consciousness (mindfulness) to our process. Our body–mind registers some incoming stimuli and we have the pleasant, neutral or unpleasant Feeling Tone. Our mind tries to make sense of it by using the labels and concepts it has stored away (Perceptions) and then a whole bunch of emotional associations, memories, assumptions, and automatic choices follow (Reactions). We don't pay attention to any of this.

Without bringing mindfulness to this process we set up a self-reinforcing loop. Our Reactions lead us to do things that stimulate further negative Feeling Tones, entrench warped Perceptions, and trigger further Reactions (like the negative eddy). Often what we do then is project all of this unpleasantness onto the raw data that came through our senses in the first place as if it were a quality of the person or situation out there that is to blame. We don't see that it was our own process that caused the negative eddy.

Examples

Steve Irwin, a very well-known Australian TV personality, was an adventurer and was often filmed wrestling crocodiles. Steve died while being filmed under water as he approached a stingray. The stingray obviously felt threatened and hit him with the poisonous barb in its tail. By the time they got Steve to the surface he was dead.

This incident opened my eyes to how many people loved him, especially men. At the time I was conducting a leadership program which involved very open, personal one-on-one meetings with the program participants. All of the participants were men, mostly of the 'man's man' variety.

In these meetings several participants divulged to me that they were quite devastated at the loss of this man. He was a flamboyant character and to me seemed entertaining and a bit over-the-top, likeable, but I didn't take him very seriously. I discovered that many of these men felt differently. They loved this guy!

In the weeks after this incident there were news reports of some Steve Irwin fans, young men, going about killing stingrays as revenge. This was a classic case of taking what was their own difficult feelings and, rather than dealing with the grief they felt, projecting the quality of 'evil' onto stingrays as a justification to 'act out' their upset.

That is, they didn't have the courage to hold their seat and feel what they felt; they attempted to discharge those difficult feelings by blaming the species that killed their hero. That's reactivity.

Another example: I'm walking down the street with my English friend. In the dry leaves next to us, something moves. I turn to look at it, hoping to see a lizard. My friend jumps three feet into the air in fright, thinking it's a snake.

I had a positive Feeling Tone. My Perception, based on the sound, was that there was probably a cute little lizzie scurrying about and I felt drawn to see it. My friend had a negative Feeling Tone, based on the Perception that it was a snake, because among her Reactions was a belief that Australia is full of dangerous venomous things that kill you.

This is what it means to 'own our feelings' - to see the reality that our feelings are the product of internal conditions (our Feeling Tones, Perceptions and Reactions) and external conditions (sound waves) coming together. The sound waves didn't cause the feelings. If that were true, I would have been scared too when the leaves rustled.

It's the combination of the external conditions meeting with our internal conditions that gave rise to the feelings. While we don't have control over all our internal conditions (many are things we've 'learnt' from our past before we had insight or awareness), they are a characteristic of our body–mind, not the external event.

If my friend brought mindfulness (Consciousness) to this situation and looked at it closely, her understanding might mean that next time she hears the leaves rustle she mightn't jump quite as high. Her Feeling Tone would be less strongly unpleasant and her Perceptions might incorporate the knowledge that short sharp sounds like that are lizard sounds, not snake sounds, and that lizards are incredibly common in the suburbs whereas snakes are not. This might lead to a different Reaction.

If she doesn't bring any mindfulness to the situation, she'll be well prepared to take up high jump.

Can you see how Reactions, allowed to run unchecked, can reinforce Perceptions and Feeling Tones? We add fuel to the fire in the Reactions cluster. Our unconscious reactions are to push away pain when we feel an unpleasant Feeling Tone (like the stingray slayers) and to gorge on pleasures when we feel a pleasant one.

In the lizard scenario, the damage done from an automatic 'pushing away' was negligible (just a little embarrassment at having been scared of a harmless creature). However when we look at the more common and less obvious reactive habits in the Reactions bucket, we'll see that they can be extremely harmful.

Holding our seat in discomfort

The challenge is to bring mindfulness (in the Consciousness cluster) to this process so that we can see the mechanics of our own dramas being created. However, our mind takes the shape of what we rest it on. So being with the unpleasant process we've whipped up here makes us feel … unpleasant. We react by avoiding it somehow.

Instead, we need to learn to hold our seat in discomfort, to be with it. Think of a rider on a horse-in-training. The horse is skittish and scared of the new experience of having a human on its back. It's flighty and it bucks.

A skilled rider can hold their seat, that is, stay in the saddle, even though the horse is bucking around. Psychologists call this 'distress tolerance', the willingness to experience discomfort rather than 'act out' (like killing stingrays) to get rid of the unpleasantness.

We're talking about reversing an ingrained habit. A well-known trajectory for learning to do something new is summarised as:

1. unconscious incompetence → 2. conscious incompetence → 3. conscious competence → 4. unconscious competence

If this is the first time you've thought about the idea of dismantling your reactivity rather than letting it rip, you'll be starting from the first box. That is, you didn't even know you hadn't developed the skill of dismantling reactivity.

If you've come across the idea before and have had time to see your habits of running from and fighting unpleasantness, but haven't yet started to change them, you're in box 2.

As soon as you start building your willingness and ability to dismantle reactivity by turning and facing unpleasantness rather than running from or fighting it, you're heading for box 3. You'll be in box 3 when you've solidified your skills and willingness to approach unpleasantness but you still have to consciously work at it.

When you reach box 4, the skill has become a natural thing for you.

This little story, from An Autobiography in Five Parts by Portia Nelson brings this alive nicely.

1) I walk down the street.

There is a deep hole in the footpath.

I fall in.

I am lost …

It isn't my fault.

It takes forever to find a way out.

2) I walk down the same street.

There is a deep hole in the sidewalk.

I pretend I don't see it.

I fall in again.

I can't believe I'm in the same place.

But it isn't my fault.

It still takes a long time to get out.

3) I walk down the same street.

There is a deep hole in the sidewalk.

I see it is there.

I still fall in … it is a habit.

My eyes are open.

I know where I am.

It is my fault.

I get out immediately.

4) I walk down the same street.

There is a deep hole in the sidewalk.

I walk around it.

5) I walk down another street.

Before we look more closely at common reactive habits and the problems they cause, I want to describe two essential attitudes to bring to this kind of personal work.

The first is compassion. I like Portia's story because it reminds me that everyone knows this territory of realising we've got unhelpful habits and struggling to change them. This is challenging and courageous work, and we need to be gentle and compassionate and patient with ourselves as we do it. We don't set out to create these unhelpful habits, they just arise as part of being the creatures that we are.

Secondly, we need curiosity. This is a top-quality replacement for judgment (which is not terribly compassionate) and for assumptions. At its heart, the Second Great Task is the willingness to walk toward unpleasantness with the question, 'What is this?', or 'What's going on here?' and see our own unpleasant patterns as subjects to be explored.

Two reactive habits: fight and flight

The two common ways that we resist unpleasantness and fuel our reactivity line up pretty nicely with the instinctual fight and flight responses to threat.

The themes of your mental movies are a good clue as to which response is more of a habit for you. As you read these movie themes, see if you recognise one as more familiar than the other.

The fight habit: You force some kind of change to occur; perhaps taking matters into your own hands and dishing out some kind of revenge, criticism, judgment, lesson or punishment to someone else. Maybe you're sorting someone out verbally or maybe even aggressing physically; perhaps you explode at people or use stern tones of voice and body language to scare them into submission. Maybe you're pretending you're more certain about things than you really are, or being very black and white about an issue.

This tendency also includes the covert fight habits (often called passive aggression) where we undermine or sabotage someone behind the scenes, perhaps manipulate them, exclude or ostracise them, try and destroy their reputation when they're not around, or other forms of non-confrontational damage.

The flight habit: We're distracting ourselves from the situation somehow, perhaps walking away, avoiding disagreement, getting drunk or high, putting a positive spin on it that's not really genuine, engaging in constant activity, company, or consumption. Media consumption is a particularly common distraction in our societies (movies, TV, internet, social media).

This tendency also includes automatically pleasing others, even when it's to our own detriment. We avoid thinking or talking about stressful situations: the distractions help our avoidance.

There's another Flight movie that looks a lot like a Freeze movie, but it's not. In this movie we're playing a victim who is hard done by and has no choice. Usually the audience is feeling sorry for us. Perhaps someone in the movie comes and helps us, cares for us or soothes us somehow. The theme is usually that someone (or life) has treated us unfairly or badly, we're suffering and someone else comes and fixes things.

What we're really fleeing from is the power we have to change things. We want someone else to do it. Blaming others and resenting them while we wait for justice can be a way of discharging our difficult feelings in the meantime. We're familiar with righteous anger about what others 'should' be doing.

For the sake of completeness, there's also a third type of response to threat, the freeze habit. This is a state of shut-down where we are so overwhelmed that we can't act. It's often associated with trauma, although not exclusively. It refers to any situation where we feel so overwhelmed that we can't respond.

This habit is harder to change on our own because of the state of overwhelm; in the case of trauma, professional help is usually required. It's also different in that it's not aversion to unpleasantness - in fact in this state, we're stuck in it.

Our inner Davey Jones

Many of our reactive habits revolve around the need to be included, to belong. We are social beings and we need to feel connected as much as we need to eat and drink. Anyone who says they don't care about what others think of them is exaggerating. People vary in the extent to which they let the need for connection drive their decisions, but it's a fundamental human need.

A character that vividly embodies the pain paradox with psycho–social unpleasantness is Davey Jones from the *Pirates of the Caribbean* movies. Davey Jones was in love with the ocean spirit Calypso. But the spirit of the ocean is to be free, so she left him. This broke his heart. It hurt so much that in order to avoid the pain he cut out his heart, put it in a box and buried it so that he never has to feel the hurt of heartbreak again.

As a result of this attempt to avoid pain, he turns into a cruel and hideous monster who, having cut off his own feelings, spends the rest of his life terrorising and killing sailors at sea, the very people to whom he was meant to be giving safe passage. The knock-on effects of his unwillingness to feel his own pain, to tolerate his own distress at a moment in time, are terror and destruction for thousands of people.

While for most of us, the knock-on effects aren't quite as dramatic as this, there are two important things to realise about our garden-variety reactive habits. First, while they may not be extreme, they create unnecessary hurt for ourselves and the beings we love.

At first glance that kind of statement can sound motherhood-ey. I think it's important to find a way to tune in to this, to really feel the care you have for your life and for other beings. Anything that reminds you of your temporariness is helpful on this front.

Something that works for me is the song *Last Day on Earth* by Kate Miller-Heidke. It's about the world coming to an end and the person she loves but is no longer with, returns to be with her. It's an emotive song and whenever I hear it I imagine standing there as the world crumbles around me with my husband (and dog) feeling deeply sad about the time we spent arguing or being unkind to one another. In fact I feel sad about every act of unkindness. At the same time my heart is lifted by the love and kindness that I've received and given.

Meditating on death is another good technique. Whatever does it for you, it's really helpful to find a way to feel honestly the reality of creating hurt and pain.

The second important thing to grasp about our not-so-dramatic hunger-feeding habits is that they are exactly the same process as the Davey Jones scenario. At any point in time at multiple places around the world, political and other group leaders feed their hungers through power and force, leading to death, torture, deprivation and desperation for large numbers of beings.

For example I read an Amnesty International campaign for a ten year old Afghani girl who was raped. The rapist had been apprehended but her family wanted to kill her for bringing shame on the family - an 'honour killing'. Their desire for belonging to their group was so strong that they would kill their own traumatised daughter. At the extremes, reactive hunger-feeding results in untold amounts of suffering.

It's easy to sit back and criticise these people for the harm they are doing. But what happens when we recognise that we are doing exactly the same thing on a smaller scale? Ghandi's attitude arises for me here: Be the change you want to see.

Our inner Cookie Monster

I've been talking a lot so far about aversion - the unwillingness to be with the unpleasant. But what about the other type of hunger - clinging or grasping - the desperate desire to keep the pleasant things going at all costs?

These two processes are part of the same impulse, two sides of the same coin. Let's say I suffer from the reactive habit of constantly surrounding myself with other people, a compulsive need for company. Blank spaces in the diary are not okay.

If we look closely we see that it's actually aversion to a pleasure ending. I see the trailer for the mental movie called *The Party's Over* or *Being on my Own* and there's an unpleasant Feeling Tone. So I do my best to ensure the cookie supply (in this case interpersonal pleasure) continues without interruption. Can you see how the grasping at pleasure and the running from pain are two sides of the same coin?

Sometimes grasping after pleasure is in the foreground and more obvious; sometimes aversion from pain is more prominent. They are essentially the same thing: they are a reaction that rejects the experience I'm having right now and desperately reaches for a different one.

Gotama identified a number of things that trigger a lot of reactivity. They're often called the *Eight Worldly Winds*:

Pleasure and pain

Praise and blame

Loss and gain

Obscurity and fame

If you think about it, a heck of a lot of our reactive aversion is to pain, blame (or criticism), loss and obscurity (or not being seen/ attended to). And much of what we reactively chase is pleasure, praise (e.g. social media likes and compliments), gain and fame (or notoriety).

I'll keep referring to the reactive habits generally as the Davey Jones and Cookie Monster strategies as an easy memory aid.

The cost of pain-relief: numbness

The other unhelpful symptom of the Davey Jones strategy (besides creating a heap of pain for himself and others) is that he personally lost connection with his own emotional world, numbing it by locking away his heart and then acting out as a tyrant.

Brené Brown is one of my favourite speakers, and in researching shame she discovered the importance of embracing vulnerability to living a whole-hearted life. She talks about shopping, drugs and alcohol as ways we numb ourselves to vulnerability; some other less obvious numbing agents are certainty and blame. As we've seen, these are all reactive habits.

As Brown says, you can't selectively numb. The more you numb your vulnerable shades of emotion the more you numb it all. It's the same with weight loss: you can't selectively lose fat from your belly or thighs, you have to take the approach of shedding it from your whole body. I you numb yourself to your vulnerable feelings you also numb yourself to the range of joyful feelings including connection with others.

To build the reality of unpleasantness into our view of life and to get to know it (First Great Task) requires us to see, expect and accept it. To dismantle our reactive habits (Second Great Task) requires us to stop running towards the pleasant and away from the unpleasant, and to cultivate a willingness to be with both. This requires us to have the distress tolerance to get curious about our hunger for things to be different and our reactions to that, rather than moving into the automatic reactive pattern of avoid-pain/chase-pleasure.

Because we use the avoid-pain/chase-pleasure principle, we never stop and look our pain in the eye to see what it really is and how it works. We do a Davey Jones. And give birth to our demons.

By demons I simply mean the things that scare us (e.g. powerlessness, disconnection). Because we haven't found any other ways to deal with these fears, our reactions draw on the protective mechanisms from the past that have made us feel safer in some way, behaviours from the avoid-pain/chase-pleasure menu. The more we use them, the more entrenched they become. We don't even realise we're doing it - the stage of unconscious incompetence.

Next in the process of dismantling reactivity, the Second Great Task, we'll move from unconscious incompetence to conscious incompetence. Let's look closely at our reactive habits to build an awareness of what we're doing currently that's not working so well for us.

The detail: some reactive (pain-relief) behaviours

Our reactive habits are insidious. They're so well practised that often we don't even see them. To bring this alive, I've listed some common examples of reactivity from our modern lifestyles that may not spring immediately to mind.

In each of these cases, we are using our behaviour to fight off a fear (unpleasant feeling) rather than face it; we are trying to avoid the feeling of unpleasantness rather than having the distress tolerance to hold our seat, to be with it.

Some corresponding fears are also offered. I'm not suggesting that all people who act in these ways are driven by these fears - there can be other drivers. However I've found these patterns between the reactive behaviours and the fears to be common.

Table 4: Fears that can drive reactive habits

Reactive habit	(Unpleasant) fears that can drive it
You have a bad reaction to people challenging or disagreeing with you, or you spend a lot of time instructing others even when not in the role of 'teacher'.	You may have learnt that to be wrong is to be worthless, and to be right and knowledgeable is to be valuable.
You always have to be working on a goal and you feel unhappy whenever you are not achieving something.	You may have learnt that in order to be approved of or wanted, you have to be useful or good at things. In some cases this can instead be an addiction to the satisfaction or even thrill of achievement.
You spend a lot of energy trying to please others and get very upset if ever someone is unhappy with you.	You may have learnt that to be wanted you must please people and make them feel good. You're afraid that if someone is unhappy with you they might sever their connection with you.
You put great emphasis on prizes and awards. You get down in the dumps if ever you lose a competition. You don't like to think about, acknowledge or talk about failures.	You may have learnt that to be of worth or relevance you must be respected and admired. You have a belief that awards are an indisputable sign that you are worthy of respect and admiration regardless of your flaws. For you, winning brings respect and admiration and losing brings your worth into question.
You insist on things being perfect and get irritated when your staff (or spouse, or children) don't do things perfectly.	You may have learnt that perfection earns you respect and admiration. Whatever your other faults may be, if you can do things perfectly, you'll be valuable and therefore acceptable. To be imperfect jeopardises this respect and admiration.

Reactive habit	(Unpleasant) fears that can drive it
You blame or criticise people for being at fault, for being the cause of the difficulty.	You may have learnt that being flawed brings your worth into question. If the unpleasantness is someone else's fault your worth will be safe.
You talk incessantly about yourself.	You may be afraid that you don't matter, that you're not seen, recognised, or valued by others. So you constantly seek others' attention to stave off feelings of invisibility and irrelevance.
You avoid people who are weak, nervous, self-doubting, overweight, less intelligent or in any way unattractive.	You may see these characteristics as undesirable and fear that being connected with such people would mean others might associate you with them and therefore not want to be associated with you.
You make sure you are always busy and go nuts if you don't have anything to do.	You may not like the discomfort that arises when your inner world is given space to be heard. This is often driven by repressed and unaddressed inner turmoil. You're afraid of facing this.
You spend a lot of time daydreaming about the future or reminiscing about your past rather than being present to your current circumstance.	You may be dissatisfied with your life as it is and avoid that unpleasantness by allowing your mind to inhabit the excitement of possibility from The Future mental movie, or reliving highlights from The Past mental movie.

Reactive habit	(Unpleasant) fears that can drive it
You're only happy when you've got other people around.	You may doubt that others value you, so you constantly seek reassurance through social interaction. Or you might be avoiding your inner world which feels like an uncomfortable place of turmoil.
You think and speak as if things are black and white; as if you're 100% certain of things all the time	Uncertainty might make you feel vulnerable and you don't like that uncomfortable feeling. So you try to convince yourself and others that the world is clearly cut into right/wrong, good/bad, worthy/unworthy, in/out and that there are no shades of grey. This might also give you a sense of control and safety as you 'know the enemy'.

Can you see what I mean by our reactive habits being insidious? It's not immediately obvious that these patterns are pain-relief strategies - ways of reacting to feed our hunger for our present experience to be different than it is, of not showing up for what's here (the unpleasant feeling) but of getting rid of it or transferring it somehow.

The first eight of these are variants on the fear of exclusion due to worthlessness. Fear around the needs for connection and belonging is a vulnerability for many of us these days. It drives a lot of reactivity.

You might recognise your own tendencies from those descriptions. Maybe you operate across several reactive habits but some might be more practised than others.

The problem with common pain-relief strategies

These pain-relief strategies are quite blunt instruments. While they make us feel a bit safer or happier in the moment, they create other pain and fear in the process. Indeed some of these pain-relief strategies cause obvious harm.

In addition to causing harm, they distract us from dealing with our own reality. If we discharge our unpleasant feelings in these or other ways before having been present to our experience, the pain will return at some point, looking scarier than it did last time. If we attend to it fully, we become more aware of our own patterns; this awareness loosens their grip on us next time we encounter them.

Once we've seen, accepted, understood and really felt all the feelings in our reactive pattern, the pattern starts to lose its power. The more we bring mindfulness to our reactivity, the more that reactivity changes. Indeed mindfulness (not necessarily meditation) is a key tool used in dealing with Post-Traumatic Stress Disorder (PTSD), an extreme case of reactivity.

So next time you have a strong unpleasant feeling, a tinge of distress of some kind, think about Davey Jones and ask yourself, 'Can I hold my seat and have my humanity? Instead of separating from my feelings, instead of dampening, closing off from or trying to destroy this experience, can I invest in building my own distress tolerance and know it? What mind activity is present? What are the real feelings underneath? How does it feel in the body? And how do these aspects of my experience change as I hold my seat in the middle of it?'

Being with unpleasantness changes it

For those who like a bit of academic proof, there is good scientific evidence for the minimisation of physical pain through knowing, accepting and being with it. An excellent practice called Mindfulness Based Stress Reduction (MBSR) was pioneered by Jon Kabbat-Zin with psoriasis patients in hospitals. As the symptoms of psoriasis are skin lesions, it's easy to measure its severity. The treatment for psoriasis involves exposing the skin to UV light so these patients had to spend time in UV capsules, a fairly unpleasant experience.

Kabbat-Zin led an experiment where one group of patients was taught mindfulness meditation which they practised during their treatments. This involved paying attention to the experience they were having: the mind activity, the emotions that arose, and the body sensations (a bit like using the Five Clusters: in fact MBSR is based on the dharma). The other group could let their minds do whatever they naturally did during the treatment.

The results were remarkable with the mindfulness group showing a marked decrease in the number of skin lesions. This showed in a clear and measurable way that intimacy with and acceptance of unpleasantness has an impact. It reduces the optional unpleasantness that's self-created through our mind activity, which in turn benefits our physical being. The research that's continued since then confirms the benefits of this kind of mindfulness for many difficulties.

I've had countless examples from my own life where facing unpleasantness has disempowered my demons, the things that were scaring me.

Example

At the age of 45 I discovered the event I was best at in athletics, the 400 m hurdles. Two years later I'd become the World Champion in my age group, broken the Australian record twice and come within 0.79 of a second of the World Record. I decided I really wanted to reach my full potential with this and so I set my sights on the only box I hadn't yet ticked - breaking the World Record.

I was confident I could do it. In my best run I'd been a bit too close to some hurdles which robbed me of momentum and energy (as I had to re-accelerate after each one) and added time. I was still quite new to the event, the most technical of all track events, and I didn't really feel I'd mastered how to run it.

I decided to pull out all stops and the following year was lucky to have Jana Pittman agree to coach me: Jana was two times World Champion, four times Commonwealth Games gold medallist, and Olympian in this event. If anyone could teach me how to run it, she could. I took on the training load of a full-time athlete, training six days a week, sometimes twice a day, and getting seriously fit and fast. That World Record was looking like toast!

Five weeks before World Championships, disaster struck. I was bitten by the wrong mosquito and contracted Ross River Virus. I was hit by dizziness and fatigue. I could barely walk up the stairs let alone run the 400 m hurdles. There was nothing I could do. I just had to wait for my body to build up an immunity.

That marked the beginning of an 18-month roller coaster ride. I didn't break the World Record at World Champs, and came home with a bronze medal. The next few months saw some recovery, only for the virus to reactivate just in time for World Indoor Champs in Poland the following year. I under-performed again. With just nine months left in my five-year age group I got back on the horse and tried once more.

Another few months of training and, with just four months left, I was ready for my first race post-recovery. At training the day before, the fatigue came back AGAIN. It hit me. I had to accept that it was now unlikely I'd achieve this goal I'd worked so hard for. Feelings of grief began to appear. This led to a powerful experience of facing unpleasantness.

I went home and used journaling to coach myself through the process of facing my pain, to really look at it, understand it, and see what it was about. On one level it's obvious - missing out on something I'd worked really hard for over a long period of time. But it was more than that. There was attachment in there, a very emotional sense of loss which was more than just not achieving something I'd worked for.

As I did this, I discovered some real pain around the sense of missing out. I have a talent but as a kid, the second of six children, with the family that I had, I missed out on having that talent encouraged and nurtured. At the age of 14 I'd received a letter from Flinders University Athletics Club asking if I'd join them to train for the 400 m hurdles. I was a bit scared and it would have involved logistical hassle – we lived 3 km from the nearest bus stop. My parents gave no encouragement and did nothing to help me get past that. The ship sailed without me.

It was wonderful to have the opportunity to do that later in my life when I no longer needed parental support. But now, after coming so close, that ship was about to sail too. In four months' time I would turn 50, my long hurdles distance would drop to 300 m, and the opportunity to do my best at this event would be gone. Again!

Over the course of about three hours I faced all of this honestly and openly. It was like a weight was lifted from me. There was still a little sadness present, but I wasn't stuck in it. It was just one feature of a much bigger picture. At the start of that session I rated my stress as an 8.5 out of 10. At the end of it, I rated it a 3.

There was no happy ending to this story. Despite being very fit and totally capable of achieving it, I continued to be hit by inexplicable fatigue over the remaining four months. Two weeks before turning 50 I decided to give up the chase. I think of my body as a good friend and it was trying its hardest to give me what I wanted but there was something wrong. I felt like a bad friend for ignoring that and insisting that we continue.

It got worse. I decided I needed to figure out what was wrong so that after a well-earned break, I could resume training without worrying. It turns out that over the last few months of my World Record campaign, I was simply not eating enough. Not enough energy coming in for the energy going out and for recovery from each session. I'd just taken my eye off the ball with my diet!

In the place I was staying I had no bathroom scales or full length mirror to see that I'd become so lean, so it just didn't occur to me. I'd done all the hard work for nearly three years, been resilient and tenacious despite setbacks, and in the end I failed because I took my eye off of something as basic as my diet.

That could have been devastating. But I wasn't devastated. Sad, yes, and incredulous. But by the time this was revealed, I'd fully faced that demon and it no longer threw me off track.

This is dharma practice in action. And in fact I've turned this process into a service using messaging apps as the communication tool (which works fabulously!). Typically my clients report a 40–50% reduction in stress from just one 90 minute session of facing their unpleasantness! That's usually enough to strip out the overwhelm and allow them to harness their own talents and courage to start dismantling the reactivity as they move forward.

I'll offer you some instructions for a simple *demon tea-party* shortly, but first, we already have one tool in our kit for bringing mindfulness to any situation.

The Five Clusters as a mindfulness tool

Let's re-visit for a moment the Five Clusters. These are five elements of our experience, a way of breaking it down so that we can attend to it closely. To remind you, they are:

Body Sensations: the five physiological senses plus the mind; our sensorium.

Feeling Tones: the general tone of pleasant, unpleasant or neutral that imbues every experience.

Perceptions: the way we recognise, name and label things in our world; the knowledge and concepts attached to our sense data.

Reactions: thoughts and emotions associated with these sensations and concepts; the 'stuff' that comes up automatically from our body–mind in response to the experience e.g. memories, habitual thoughts and feelings, underlying beliefs, our patterns of association and automatic responses as well as our deliberate responses.

Consciousness: the conscious awareness of any of the above and the mental activity we conjure or allow in response to that awareness.

In a general sense, these clusters move from automatic and unconscious elements of our experience to more conscious elements over which we can exercise choice. This gives us a clue about the easiest place to start if we want to change our habits - the place where we have the most awareness and the most choice. I'm going to use the Consciousness cluster as you read this to focus on the Perceptions and Reactions clusters.

The Perceptions cluster is our understanding of what the incoming data is - what we recognise it to be. For example, that sound is rain on the roof, or those words are criticism. The Reactions cluster is our reactions to what we perceive is there - memories, associations, feelings, habitual narratives, and what we actually do in response.

Perception sets us up for Reaction. For example you say something about me and I perceive it to be criticism, whereas my friend sitting next to me didn't recognise it that way. That sets off Reactions in me because I have a sensitivity to criticism, whereas my friend, even when she does perceive criticism coming her way, doesn't get as upset.

Our Perceptions of incoming data are affected by our history, what we've encountered before; our Reactions are what happens as a result also affected by our history). Perception is often outside our awareness, but it is our Reactions cluster that bridges the divide between these unconscious automatic Perceptions and our Consciousness (awareness). Bringing Consciousness to both clusters can yield profound insight. Remember dharma practice has two parts: serenity and insight - this is a practice for the latter.

Let's look at another example to work this through, an example of resistance to unpleasantness through reactively feeding the hunger for things to be different. We'll use it to take a close look at the Perceptions and Reactions clusters: my patterns of perception and the thoughts and feelings that follow. This time it's in a work setting.

I'm running my business and I'm snowed under with work. Several things have gone wrong in the past six months which have caused my workload to increase. I'm pretty happy with the way I've dealt with these difficulties, having managed to stay calm, accept that these things have happened and get on with doing what I had to do.

I finally decide that it's time for me to hire someone to help out. I've been putting it off because it will actually be more work to keep the wheels turning AND recruit, select, hire and train a new person, but I finally decide that a few weeks of even MORE work is worth the long-term benefit.

So for a few weeks I'm burning the midnight oil, struggling a bit with the lack of headspace and the constancy of work, but I keep putting one foot in front of the other. I write the job ad, post it, spend hours wading through resumes (feeling a little annoyed at the scattergun job applicants), compile a shortlist, email those who didn't make it, organise some competency testing for the shortlisted candidates and an interview time for each, write up my interview questions, all the time communicating with them to keep them enthusiastic, and then interview the four on the shortlist.

Only one is suitable. Fortunately she's the one who's been expressing a desire to keep things moving quickly as she's very keen to start. We make her an offer which she accepts.

Three days later she pulls out.

I lose the plot.

If we start with Reactions in this scenario, that is, my reactive mental activity when the candidate pulled out, it went something like this:

'You are $%*&^% kidding me! I cannot believe this is happening! I've done a good job of being calm through lots of challenges lately, it's time things went right for once. I've risen to the challenge of these testing times, it's about time I had a smooth run. I have two choices now, either more of the same over-work or to go through this whole process again which is even more work. This is never going to end!'

Reactions are the habits of mind, emotion and reaction that arise automatically in response to our Perceptions of what's going on. Can you spot some habits of mind? Some assumptions and beliefs about the world perhaps?

You may have spotted the underlying belief in some ubiquitous sense of justice - the idea that if I deal well with things for a certain amount of time, then the universe will deliver me a smooth run. This was a belief embedded in my Perception of the situation being out of balance or unfair. This led to a Reaction of a catastrophic mental movie playing in my mental cinema, the *It'll Never End* movie. (Psychologists call this *catastrophising*.)

This example points to an intellectual implication of the First Great Task: if we truly understand and accept that life contains stuff that we don't want, we will expect it. Our ever-present assumption would be 'anything can happen any time'.

I mentioned that things had gone wrong in the time leading up to this event and I was feeling good about how calmly I'd dealt with it. Part of that was genuinely because I'd viewed it through the lens of the First Great Task - I expected that things would go wrong because that's the nature of things and so I'd been having a very different emotional experience up until then.

After this little episode I discovered something that was buried in my Perceptions: my automatic beliefs about things led to my perception that events were ridiculously misaligned with normality. I was expecting a certain amount of things to go wrong. Probability says that it's uncommon to have many instances of things going 'wrong' all in a row. I had indeed adjusted my expectations of life to include things going 'wrong', but in a statistically probable measure! Clearly that measure had just been exceeded, which led to me losing the proverbial plot.

Instead of integrating into my expectations the ever-present likelihood of undesirable stuff, I'd integrated the ever-present likelihood of an equal amount of undesirable and desirable stuff. I'd adjusted my expectations for the fact that the desirable and undesirable might not occur in equal frequency in any given week or month. But that in any given six-month period I believed I should see a pretty good dose of the desirable stuff. It wasn't until that expectation was transgressed that I realised this was an automatic and uninspected belief that arose as part of my Perception of the situation that led to my Reactions to it.

Psychologist Jonathan Haidt talks about how we often use the analogy of a car when we're talking about orienting our way through life. Know where you are, set the course for where you want to be, and then navigate your way there - all very simple and straightforward.

However life's not like that. Because animals were more common vehicles in days of old, Haidt suggests that this helped people stay in tune with the fact that they were not in complete control of their lives. Animals have their own fears and desires, and using animals for transport was a less predictable way of getting from A to B than our modern cars. In fact a spooked elephant (a historical version of the armoured tank) could be very dangerous to its own army, turning around and running straight through its own troops!

Haidt suggests that the amount of control we have over such animals is probably more reflective of the reality of our lives. We might want to get from A to B but things may or may not turn out that way. We may or may not get to where we want to go in the time frame we set for ourselves - or ever!

With our lives so individualised and seemingly controllable these days, we can forget that in fact we live in a swirling universe of many causes and effects, some of which we brush up against and some of which we don't. Our own actions are important, but they are just one of the gazillion things going on. This belief about life is a much more helpful one than 'I'm in control, it's my life and I'll have it go exactly the way I choose, when I choose it'.

As the First Great Task tells us, if we can truly expect unpleasantness in our future, we'll find that some of the stress that occurs when things go wrong subsides. We might still feel some stress (less as we practise it more) but we don't multiply it with fury and a sense of injustice. If we accept that things don't go right and expect them to not go right in the future, we'll be much less surprised and resentful when they do … not go right.

If this expectation had been in my beliefs about life, it would have affected my Perception of the situation with this scenario (it would have just seemed normal) and there would have been less splash and spray in the pool (my little melt-down Reaction).

Unhelpful and inaccurate beliefs come in myriad forms, ready to trigger Reactions to sensory data. Particularly insidious are generic faulty beliefs about our worth or love-ability as a person. These range from 'Nobody really loves me' to 'Unless I'm an outstanding success I won't be loveable' to 'I'm a worthless individual who deserves to be treated badly' or 'I'll only be accepted if I follow the rules and do the right thing'.

Of course there are far worse ones too, such as the belief that victims of sexual assault are responsible for it. At the time of writing US President Donald Trump is about to be impeached (again), this time for inciting the violent invasion of the US Capitol building as the election results (confirming his loss) were being ratified. I suspect a faulty (and certainly unhelpful) belief driving his behaviour might be something like: 'I always get what I want' - a far cry from 'anything can happen any time'. There are many of them, they distort our experience of reality and drive us to harmful action.

For a very long time, the psychology profession has known the importance of beliefs. The well-known approach of cognitive therapy identifies faulty beliefs and often then sets about testing reality to disprove them.

Gotama spoke of 'mind' as including emotions. From an experiential point of view, thoughts and feelings appear to arise simultaneously. With advances in science however, we've been able to discover that the thought comes first - about 6/100ths of a second later, the emotions kick in. But of course the emotions then also affect subsequent thought, as we know with the negative eddy. Either way, thoughts are an important element to work with.

So let's have a look at some particularly problematic and misguided beliefs (other than those about our worthlessness) we often carry with us that affect our Perceptions and create a lot of unnecessary angst in our Reactions.

Three tragic misunderstandings

Gotama himself pointed out three characteristics of reality that we often fail to integrate into our beliefs about the world. Our failure to recognise them results in three tragic misunderstandings. And at the heart of these misunderstandings are some faulty beliefs that cause a heck of a lot of pain.

These beliefs are faulty in that they don't correspond with reality. This is not a religious-truth claim, it's simply a description of real life. You can check it out for yourself from your own life. It might be helpful to think of them as three extremely common and extremely unhelpful faulty beliefs about life that lead to heaps of unpleasantness. Let's have a look at them in turn.

Faulty belief 1: People and things offer indelible happiness

(**Gotama's characteristic:** *dukkha*)

As we know the dharma doesn't deny that lots of fun can be had in life: the pleasures we can seek are boundless, and there's nothing inherently wrong with them. The problem is we expect more from them than they can give.

Psychologists call this 'hedonic adaptation'. That is, we adapt to pleasures very quickly and they stop pleasing us. So we reactively reach for another one to try and keep the pleasure-train going. The result is we end up on a 'hedonic treadmill', always having to find another hit of pleasure and another. It's in our nature as humans to do this, so we need to see through the faulty belief that people and things outside of us are in any way reliable sources of pleasure or joy.

We all know that material things give us only a fleeting sense of joy. As human beings we have an incredible capacity to *habituate* to things, that is, to get used to them and no longer appreciate them. You only need to think about the last lot of clothes you gave away to charity and how excited you were about buying them a few years ago. This isn't a problem. We just need to see it and stop expecting something different.

Another example is our relationships. They can provide us with lots of good feelings: intimacy, security, self esteem, a sense of being important and cared about, safety. Who would deny these are positive things? Indeed many studies show that social connectedness and intimacy are two strong predictors of our sense of happiness, wellbeing, and even our physical health and longevity. This makes sense because, as we know, the needs for connection and belonging are wired into our DNA

However, Gotama tried to tell us that the good feelings resulting from satisfying our needs and enjoying the pleasures of life pale in comparison to the joy, peace, calm, friendliness and contentment that come with an awakened mind.

In contrast, those wonderful feelings from relationships depend on certain people behaving in certain ways, as well as us being in certain mental and emotional states. Relationships can bring us wonderful things, but they also bring challenges, difficulties and loss. These thing tend not to make it into our Perceptions about relationship.

So rather than giving us a hard time for enjoying our common pleasures, he was trying to help us see that our expectations are often out of step with reality. This gap between our expectations and realit causes us stress.

In addition, because of the second faulty belief, many of our good experiences are typified by a corresponding unpleasantness because they necessarily pass when we don't want them to. I've noticed this with my own experience in eating food. Moments after I tuck into a mouthful of a yummy meal, I find my mind flitting automatically to what's for dessert.

Eating at a sushi restaurant serving food on a conveyor belt is another example - you've only just started on your first plate of food when your eyes start scanning for what's next. The mind has anticipated the disappointment that this pleasure will end, so goes looking for the next one.

Many of our pleasures suffer from some variety of this pain. It's just in the nature of pleasures. We need to build this into our understanding and expectation of the world. We need to see through the delusion, the faulty belief.

Faulty belief 2: Some things are reliable, stable and permanent

(**Gotama's characteristic:** *anicca*, **meaning unreliable, unstable or impermanent**)

I call this the RSP delusion (reliable, stable, permanent). Most of us, if pressed, would say we don't believe that the world is reliable, stable and permanent. We only have to look at our past - our jobs, relationships, the quality of relationships, our tastes in things, even our bodies and minds have changed.

However, if we're honest, most of us have not really embraced this and incorporated it into our world view. As we found with the poster for the My Future movie, our expectations of what any given day will bring tend to assume the good things will last.

For example, we all expect that our parents will die before us. But when it happens, we often go into shock and denial. We enter the shift and the tectonic plates of our life move: a big mental adjustment takes place as we are parted from things we love.

However, it's often much greater than it would be if we truly lived each day knowing that all meetings end in separation, whether through death or other means. Because we see many endings as sad, and because we aren't great at being with the unpleasant, we often avoid even thinking about them.

Think about the things you take for granted and you'll be honing in on your RSP delusions, the areas where you might expect things to be reliable, stable and permanent. Perhaps your marriage? Your job? The government of the day (certainly not here in Australia!)? Your friendships? The lives of the people and animals you love? Your own body parts? Your own life? Your house? Your town or city in its current state, size and character?

Of course it's natural to expect that many of these things will probably be here tomorrow as they are today, but are you aware that it's 'probably', or do you expect it **will** be?

I had a vivid experience of this while I was writing this chapter. I had two chickens whom I enjoyed very much and expected would be with me for several years to come. They were very much pets and were real characters. The day before I was writing this, the temporary tenants in our house rang to tell me both hens had been attacked and killed by a dog. I felt the shift and tears came. While I didn't expect them to live as long as I expect to live myself, I did think they'd be a bit more permanent than they were.

Did you spot another piece of solid ground I've made for myself in that sentence? 'As long as I expect to live myself'. The RSP delusion is all about us trying to find some solid ground for ourselves rather than seeing ourselves as floating on an ever-changing ocean and surfing while we can.

A common meditation in the dharma is a meditation on death. If you find yourself thinking 'how depressing', it's a good sign that you are so resistant to this characteristic of life that you don't even want to think about it. Yet a beautiful thing happens when we start to allow the reality of death into our mind-scape - we start appreciating and being present to life. Often we even start appreciating those things we take for granted. The result can be a much richer appreciation of the good things we have in our lives.

A documentary called *Into the Universe with Stephen Hawking* brought the reality of the RSP delusion home to me. Hawking, one of the world's best-known cosmologists, in this documentary describes how at some point in the future, as the earth gets closer to the expanding sun, our planet will become uninhabitable. Essentially, if humans are to continue to exist, at some point we'll need to find another planet to live on. The idea of personal non-existence is one thing, but humans and all life on earth dying out? Wow! There's a dose of impermanence!

Our desire for stability is wily, sneaking in wherever it can, including in dharma circles. I've noticed that even dharma practitioners who understand, discuss and accept the principle of impermanence can have special 'carve-out' clauses for spiritual ideas that fly in the face of it.

For example, a belief in something like 'we're all essentially love'. This sounds like a nice unifying concept that treats 'being love' as a constant, a permanent, and unshakable fact, marred only by our deviations from it when we forget 'who we really are'. The ideas of rebirth and of a soul are also carve-outs, with the essence of 'me' somehow being permanent.

In his book *Culture and the Death of God*, Terry Eagleton calls these carve-outs *displaced divinities* and he includes among them Reason, Nature, the state, science, humanity, Being, and the life force among other things. It's an interesting exercise to identify for ourselves, what ultimate realities, ultimate truths or universal constants we might rest on as reliable - overtly or otherwise.

The beauty of starting to expect the unexpected in life is not only that there is less shock and grief when unreliability, instability and impermanence occur, but that we can appreciate more vividly the existence that we have, and the beings we share it with. We also start to see more clearly the things that we are clinging to and running from with our Davey Jones strategies.

The clues lie here: when you think about the impermanence of things - certain people, animals, places, experiences - what things bring about strong emotion for you? What don't you want to look at?

Faulty belief 3: 'Who I am' is a fixed, independent, enduring and congruent identity

(Gotama's characteristic: *anatta*, meaning 'not-self')

At an excellent meditation retreat I attended, the teacher Rick Hanson explained that the term self has three common meanings:

1. The physical person

2. The mentally constructed self whom we consider to be the owner of our experience and the agent of our actions (the identity we craft for ourselves and any notion of an enduring identity such as a soul)

3. Awareness (the chooser of where to place our attention).

The term not-self refers to the second meaning. It's not denying the existence of the billions of human bodies walking around the planet. It's our tendency to construct an idea of 'who I am' and then view this 'me' as internally consistent, enduring, and fixed rather than seeing our self as a dynamic process that's constantly emerging in each moment as a result of conditions inside and outside of us coming together.

When unpleasantness arises, it's the tendency to make it about 'me'. Rather than hurt or illness or loss or problems arising, as they naturally do in the process of being human in this world, it's our tendency to become 'the one who is hurt', 'the one who is ill', 'the one who is having problems with their partner', or 'the one who has lost the race'. Of course it is the physical self, the body-mind we inhabit that's experiencing these things, but do we see it as difficulty arising in the normal flow of aliveness, or do we see it as: misfortune has chosen ME!?

Because of the advances in our modern societies, most of us spend our anxious energy on social and emotional survival rather than physical survival. Most of us have a belief that unless we build and maintain an enduring, fixed idea of 'who we are', we won't prosper in our social world. So from around our teen years onwards we start to build this sense of Me and get very upset if it's ever challenged.

While this could be considered a normal, even healthy, part of development into adulthood, we take it too far. Like the raft that gets us to the other side of the stream and is then dragged around for the rest of our lives over hill and dale. We assume that because an identity was useful in a certain part our life, we must never question it and we must keep it forever.

Instead of being honest about the fact that we think, feel and behave in all sorts of ways depending on what's happening inside and outside of us at the time, we decide on certain characteristics that are Me. We get this printed up in our Me Brochure and we try to project this image out into the world. When something happens that threatens this image, we get very upset and at the extremes, very destructive.

Examples of selfing

One of the things I tried to fix into my identity as a young person was that I was fun. Often my experience would comply - I'd entertain my friends, make people laugh, be a clown - and the identity was safe

However the truth was, it depended on many things: who else was there, how much I liked them, whether they were people whose approval I wanted, not to mention my own mood and what had been going on in the hours before that moment. I remember going to a party where I didn't know how to *talk* to anyone there, let alone entertain them.

I also remember being chastised by my family because I was fun and happy when talking to my friends but moody and unfriendly at home. So at times I was fun and entertaining, and at times I wasn't.

The problem is that because I wanted fun in the Me identity, if ever I failed to entertain or be seen as fun, I'd feel upset, disappointed; I'd feel like a failure, a nobody, or a fake. And that was just me threatening my own identity! If someone else accused me of failing to live up to the Me Brochure, look out! I'd feel quite worthless and sometimes cover that up with aggression towards that person. You can imagine how well it went down when my siblings or parents drew attention to the un-fun version of Me and proclaimed this as the 'real' Me.

At soccer matches in Europe the fans of the two competing teams are physically separated from each other to minimise the risk of brawls. Why do soccer fans fight each other? Because they've linked their personal identity to a soccer team. Their team opposes the other team, so they oppose the other fans. They feel victory and defeat very personally - as a part of 'who we are'.

This habit of identifying with things is insidious, even within Buddhist circles. Here it's clearly spelled out that identification is unhelpful and at odds with the teachings. Yet some people seem to have a lot invested in being seen to be a Buddhist.

Clues to this are the presence of a lot of Buddhist paraphernalia in the home, car, wallet or garden. Another clue is the tendency to get hot under the collar if Buddhist teachings or Buddhism itself are questioned. My guess is that there's some selfing going on for the Buddhists who get angry about the development of secular dharma.

I also wonder if the now-distinctive clothing and appearance of monastic Buddhists might lend itself to some secret identification tendencies. In Gotama's day, these robes were very similar to normal attire; he and his followers would cobble them together from those left at charnel grounds where dead bodies were disposed of. He and his monks would have been distinctive by the plainness of their attire, but it would have generally blended in. The equivalent in our place and time would be wearing clothes from a second-hand store; arguably, that would be more in keeping with the Buddha's approach.

I imagine it would be easy nowadays, when you stand out so much, to become attached to wearing robes. I imagine the ego could easily slip in to seeing one's self as special and enjoying the automatic respect, kindness and, in some cases, privilege that you'd be shown. It would be easy to adopt the identity of 'spiritual' into one's Me Brochure and get attached to it.

As I started to teach the dharma, I became aware of a temptation to start behaving 'like a dharma teacher'. For a woman that often includes speaking in soft tones and being effusive in empathy. It can also mean acting like you always know the answer and not admitting to one's own unawakened tendencies. I've been very mindful about making sure the ego doesn't update the Me Brochure to include *dharma teacher*. Being open about my own unawakened-ness is a huge part of moving through it. I don't want to hem myself in because of some new identity as an awakened dharma teacher who's supposed to be unaffected by reactivity.

The danger of Self vs Other

More extreme examples of selfing are strong senses of religious or national identity. The concept of a *jihad* (holy war) is identification on steroids, as were the Christian crusades. Interestingly identities don't have to differ much for this selfing to do its damage. For example the group that has killed the most Christians is other Christians who identify with a different brand of Christianity.

The Nazi regime was identification with an (imaginary) in-group - the Aryan race - and persecution of out-groups. We take this identity thing extremely seriously and can be very violent in desperately trying to keep up the appearance of the identity we've created.

The creation of in-groups and out-groups is another natural part of our human heritage, another arm of that need to belong that helped ensure our survival. Psychologists name it *social identity theory*. This theory describes the common human behaviour where we draw a line around an in-group to differentiate ourselves from an out-group. We over emphasise our differences with the out-group and over-emphasise our similarities with the in-group.

This process of 'othering' helps keep the 'us and them' mentality motoring and gives us a brief and somewhat delusional sense of safety. It also fuels all sorts of destructive behaviour, from ostracising the new girl on the basketball team, up to political manoeuvring in organisations (and governments), all the way to gang fights, persecuting people for their skin colour or sexual orientation, and ethnic cleansing.

When tendencies like this are described as natural, there's often also an attitude that if it's natural then that's the way it 'should' be. Such a nonsensical rationale can be said of pretty much anything. Just because something is natural doesn't mean it's good. Tsunamis are natural, hurricanes are natural, bushfires are natural, cancer is natural. Does that mean we should see these things as helpful or desirable? I don't think so.

Secondly, you can describe any human behaviour as natural. Whatever we human beings do, we do out of a body and mind that was born of the natural world. Again, that doesn't make all of our actions helpful or desirable.

And thirdly, the opposite experience is also natural - the joyful, open-hearted experience of feeling connected with others. Most of us know this experience even if it was fleeting. Facing difficulties together can often bring about this connectedness.

We have some Dutch friends whose parents/in-law came to visit them here in Australia. They went for a driving holiday in a motor home and found themselves trapped at Port Arthur in Tasmania, surrounded by bushfires. They told me how the local people were helping day and night with everything from the logistics of food and shelter to patiently repeating instructions from the fire brigade to people whose English wasn't great (including our friends' parents). Their parents spoke of the feelings of one-ness, of togetherness without boundaries, and how moved they were at the generosity of the locals.

I remember a similar feeling when the Olympic Games were held in Sydney in 2000. Sydney's our biggest city here in Australia with around 4 million people at the time of the Olympics. While people from bigger foreign cities often find Sydney friendly and laid back, compared to the rest of Australia it takes itself pretty seriously and can be a bit uptight.

However, the Olympics united the place. Thousands of people took time off work to be volunteer helpers and everyone everywhere, on the buses, in cafes, in the streets, had an attitude of friendliness and openness. It was a wonderful time. The big event united people in a mass open-armed welcome to people from everywhere.

You would know this feeling. Maybe it's the New Year's Eve fireworks, or the friendliness that seems to abound on Christmas Day. This is just as natural as the closed-hearted in-group/out-group tendencies. Different causes and conditions lead to it, and it's a bit more difficult to bring about because of our human mind's negativity bias. Nevertheless, it's a very natural part of being human.

Constructing an in-group of my people and an out-group of others in order to create or bolster an identity is the first step in separation. This separation leads, on both a large and small scale, to harm. At the very least it limits and deludes us about our own experience. At its worst it creates callousness and destruction on an epic scale.

This is very much an instance of the dharma going against the stream. The idea of letting go of a set idea of your identity might be weird or even frightening. And for young people it might even be impossible, as identity is one of those things that's hard to let go of if you've never really felt secure in it in the first place.

Rick Hanson points out that the *self organises around threat*. That is, when we feel threatened, the selfing process will often kick in strongly and the items in the Me Brochure that are relevant to warding off the threat will be brought to the fore.

This is really rich ground for curiosity and exploration. The antidote to selfing is simply to use wise attention and focus on what we share with others - on the common experience of being a sensitive creature in a world that has endless ways of causing us pain. To the extent that we're not willing to feel with others, there's some unpleasantness right there that we're not willing to sit with, which means food for dharma practice!

Practical Exercise: The Me Brochure - the act of selfing

Let's bring this concept of not-self into your own experience. Try this practical exercise. Take a piece of paper and divide it into three columns.

1. In the first column, list down the words you would use to finish the sentence 'I am …' You might come up with things like funny, smart, wise, caring, considerate, independent, sporty, strong, responsible, always right, in control, interesting, kind, glamorous, competent, adventurous; or maybe shy, hopeless, not very good at things, a follower - whatever comes to you (It can be an interesting exercise to then ask the people who know you well to do the same, but about you). We'll call this your *Me Brochure*.

2. In the second column, for each item, ask yourself whether there have been any times in your life when you have behaved in ways that wouldn't be fittingly described by that adjective. It's highly likely there are, so list those down.

3. In the third column, for each item where you behaved in a way that didn't fit the Me Brochure, write down an explanation of why you behaved that way.

Your explanations will likely describe certain conditions that led you to behave differently. This is the point - the way we behave at any given moment depends on many things. As Zen author Barry Magid said, '"Self" is not a single thing in a thousand disguises; it is a word for the thousand disguises themselves'. *I* am a fluid, dynamic process, not a fixed set of attributes.

One of the key principles Gotama talked about was *Dependent Arising* (sometimes called Dependent Origination): the arising of one thing depends on the presence of others, on causes and conditions. We've seen this for ourselves using The Five Clusters. We might have tendencies to behave in certain ways more often than in other ways (e.g. if I'm a raging extravert), but it's all about conditions. We are a dynamic, ever-changing process that is affected by conditions inside and outside of us, not a fixed, stable, independent, internally consistent identity.

This principle runs through the entire dharma and is so important that Gotama said that to see Dependent Arising is to see the dharma. Try starting to think of yourself as a fluid, dynamic process rather than a fixed, stable Me and observe what happens.

This identity can also stretch to an envisioned afterlife where one's soul or equivalent moves on to another plane of existence - is reborn, goes to heaven, becomes one with Atman, whatever it may be. Whether or not there is an afterlife is irrelevant to Gotama's teachings: as we've already seen, he consistently refused to answer questions about it, stating that it was a distraction from the important tasks. (Note: the idea of not-self is not directed at this issue, it's about the construction of Me.)

The thing here is not to set off on a debate about whether there is a soul of some sort, but to realise that what you believe about it is irrelevant to the dharma. As long as your belief doesn't get in the way of seeing yourself as a dynamic process here and now, then it's not an obstacle to correcting the third faulty belief.

What you could do is get curious about what effect your belief has on your life, the way you receive your experience and react or respond to it.

The Task: Dismantle reactivity

The Five Clusters are really helpful checkpoints for looking closely at our experience. We can direct our conscious thoughts (Consciousness cluster) to observe any experience in terms of the other four clusters (Body Sensations, Feeling Tones, Perceptions, Reactions).

As we see the fluidity and dependence on conditions of all of our experience, we stop seeing our Self as this fixed, enduring entity that is consistent with our Me Brochure at all times, that is completely under our own control and independent of its surroundings.

We also stop chasing certain experiences as if they would bring us lasting happiness. We see clearly that life is always in flux and any pleasure we might bring about is temporary. Indeed, Gotama called this contemplation of the Five Clusters his *lion's roar* in terms of its potential for awakening.

This observation alone can change the experience. However sometimes we need some more tools in the kit bag, especially with strong unpleasantness in the presence of which it might be particularly difficult to hold our seat.

As we become more aware of the elements of our experience, we start to see that some of our reactions consist of strong emotional memories, either positive or negative. When we come across these, it can help to have some tools on hand to help us be with it, because to seriously undermine the patterns that cause our reactive hunger-feeding habits requires us to face them.

We need insight and a truck load of courage: courage to break down the auto-emotive patterns between our Feeling Tones, Perceptions and Reactions. It takes courage because most of our unpleasant psychological experiences are based on fear. Fear is embedded in the Reactions.

Donald Hebb, considered to be the father of neuropsychology, coined the phrase *neurons that fire together wire together*. Somewhere in our past, often during our first 20 years of life, we've made some associations of fearful feelings with certain stimuli. We've wired some sensory stimuli (remember one of the six senses is mental activity) together with the neural and hormonal responses that occur when we feel fear.

In order to undo this link, we need to inspect it closely. That requires us to get up close and personal to our fears - to hold our seat in them, to fully know our unpleasant experience with our heart and gut and body as well as our head. We can't just know the terrain by discovering the map: we need to actually walk the landscape so that we know it viscerally. Learning 'about' the dharma won't change your life: living it will.

I want to offer you some strategies for grappling with the more unpleasant, maybe even scary unpleasantness and the need to feel it honestly - practical ways to 'be with it'. As it's such an important activity, I'm giving you a few different ways to remember your strategy so that you can take it with you in your daily life. Essentially, they all describe the same thing but one might resound more with you than the others. Then I'll share the detail of a practical way to actually do this.

Unpack the black bag

The first is a visual from the poet David Whyte who talks about the bits of unpleasantness that scares us as the contents of our *black bag*. It's a bag we carry around with us from our early life. Any time we have an experience that scares us somehow, zhoom, it goes straight into the black bag so that we can't see it. Rather than sitting with it in the bright daylight and looking at it closely to understand its true nature, we whip it quickly into the black bag so we don't have to feel that unpleasant feeling.

As we go through our life, the black bag gets bigger and bigger until it's so big that it's getting stuck behind us in elevator doors. If we want to undermine the grip that unpleasantness has on us, we need to have the courage to unpack the black bag in the light and get to know its contents intimately.

Invite your demon in for a tea party

Another visual comes from Gotama himself. If you read books on Buddhism, sooner or later you'll hear some story about demons. Gotama used the term *demon* to refer to those patterns that can knock us off the path.

In a similar way, I use it to mean any pattern of experience that scares us. So for some it might be the demon of loneliness, which might lead to all sorts of behaviour from overt attempts to please others to self-aggrandisement. If an opportunity comes up to make ourselves look clever or accomplished or popular, our ego, our identity, finds it really hard to resist. There are all sorts of demons, one for every type of fear of not being okay (safe, accepted, living a fulfilled life).

Gotama talked about the demon Mara (literally, the killer) who robs us of our full repertoire of creative response. (As soon as Gotama recognised him, he'd slink off, defeated.) Any pattern that really hooks us in and leaves our awareness, our mindfulness wondering what the hell just happened, probably points to a demon lurking. This is where the idea of detachment comes in. We don't want to detach from our experience, but we do want to detach from that reactive hook – the demon fear that triggers us into automatic reaction.

The visual that I love, that helps with the challenge of getting to know my difficult space, my unpleasant process, is that of sitting in my home and one of my demons comes knocking at the door. I know that knock and I know who it is, but rather than block or run (pretend I'm not home, stack a table behind the door), I open the door, I greet the demon, 'Ah, loneliness demon, you're back', and I invite him in for a cup of tea. It's not exactly enjoyable having tea with my loneliness demon but I embrace it anyway.

In my experience, once I've gotten to know him, he hangs around for a little while and then leaves of his own accord, even if I invite him to stay for dinner.

The demon's mission in life is to protect you. It thinks that keeping you scared of demons is the best way to do that. It doesn't expect to be invited in; if you do invite it in, it can be shocked and a bit shy. But getting to know the demon is the goal, so that when you do hear it rustling around outside, you're not so jumpy.

Walk through the mud puddle

The third way you could think about it is that each of our fears and hurts is like a big mud puddle sitting in front of us. We are standing on its bank feeling quite anxious about it. We spend much of our live distracting ourselves from the mud puddle; indeed we can go for long periods of time without seeing it. But we always know it's there and whenever we come across anything that feels, looks or smells like mud, we give it a wide berth.

Then at some point when we are tired of being scared, we might spend some time trying to figure out what's in the puddle. Maybe we even do figure it out and achieve an awareness of what's causing it. (This would be like reading about demons or black bags or mud puddles, and maybe identifying them at a distance.)

However to go mud puddling requires us to walk into the puddle and acquaint ourselves with its contours, to know its mud-scape intimately. It can be scary because if you haven't walked mud puddles before you can be worried that you mightn't come out. But if you're armed with courage, curiosity, compassion and mindfulness, you always come out, generally feeling much lighter.

My own demon tea party

In our modern world, many of our demons rest on beliefs we've adopted about shortcomings that indicate we are not worthy of connection and belonging. To bring this concept alive, let me share with you an example of my own demon tea party.

In my early adult life, I recognised that one of my demons was wrongness. If I was ever found to be wrong or flawed or blame-worthy in some way, it cut straight to my sense of worth. I could feel this demon lurking whenever I received criticism. It was like the veil had been drawn back and my true flawed self had been revealed. Again!

I tried shutting the windows and locking the door so that I could move on without having to face it. My way of blocking it out was to argue - something I can do very well. I'd find all sorts of evidence to show that the critic was wrong even if I felt a pang of recognition in what they were saying.

Sometimes, if I thought that person could damage the way others thought of me, I might even start pointing out their flaws to others to try to shore up my own loyalties, just in case they were telling others about my true pointless self.

I also realised at this point that I was quite critical of others so that I would be seen as worthy and admirable. It was the see-saw principle - if I put someone else down then I'll be up. I could see a scary pattern: I was starting to sound like my father, who sounded like his mother!

The problem with demons, or black bags, or mud puddles is that it's easy to think you're getting around them by closing the windows and doors, or tying the black bag shut, or walking around the mud puddle. Sometimes their noises are very faint, or that mud puddle looks like a speck in the rear-view mirror. We think we've left it behind or grown out of it.

But you realise that all you did was sit the demon down and then count the minutes until it finished its tea so you could show it to the door. Then you find that once again the demon is rustling the bushes outside the window and you're having the same jumpy reactions. You haven't re-wired the patterns at all, you've just avoided the conditions, the stimuli that trigger the fears. The next time the conditions (clusters of experience) come together, you find the fears are still there.

After a while I began to see this. I really wasn't able to take criticism at all, nor was I able to apologise for anything. That would clearly mean I'd done something that deserved criticism. And if I'd done something to deserve criticism, then to my body–mind it meant I was a bad person and I didn't deserve to be loved - tolerated maybe, but not loved. It was a terrifying thing for me to say sorry and on the first few occasions in my adult life where I mustered the courage to do it, I dissolved into tears.

As you can imagine, this didn't have a great effect on my relationships. So I knew I had a demon outside my window, and being criticised was the sound of the bushes rustling. Recognising and accepting that you have a demon scaring you is the first step.

Over time I began to see how much of a problem this was for me. I saw it was a handbrake on my learning as a human being. One of the main ways we learn and grow is to look honestly at what's going on inside of us, but I wasn't able to do that. I always had to have my 'there's nothing wrong with Lenorë' goggles on when I looked inside, which distorted reality to ensure that I didn't let the demon in … and feel worthless. Of course underneath all of this was fear around my needs for connection and belonging.

As I grasped this I wished it wasn't true - but it was and it felt completely out of my control. To take the goggles off was a very scary prospect. The truth is I didn't even know how to do it.

For me, the next step I took was relatively easy. It was figuring out intellectually, what was going on. I didn't have to look too far for the answer. I was the second of six children in a family where my father was clearly the head of the household. He also instilled in us a sense of awe towards himself - the image that he was always in control, always knowing what to do, a great singer, entertainer, horse-rider, always the winner of any family debate, always successful and admired. As he was my school principal for the first six years of my schooling, his power was very real to me.

So as kids we thought Dad was the bee's knees. The only thing was, he wasn't all that interested in children. We wanted his attention and approval, but these were very scant resources. If you showed you were particularly clever, either intellectually or practically, you might get a little whiff of approval - but it didn't happen often and it was generally short lived.

On family outings, when it was time to go home, he'd whistle loudly and yell out our names in quick succession as if calling a pack of dogs. If we didn't come immediately, there'd be trouble. He seemed to enjoy doing this in front of his friends. I hated it. To me it resembled how unseen and uncherished we were as individuals.

In addition to this, my father was quick to criticise. Not only was he quick but he was personal. If you mucked something up or showed any vulnerability you might be called 'hopeless' or one of his favourite critical terms, a 'pork chop' which meant weak and pathetic.

There was very little encouragement, and in hindsight he was a poor delegator, expecting us to know how he wanted a job done without explaining it properly, if at all. To ask a question always risked an answer delivered in a tone that felt to me like 'you stupid idiot'. I remember well the feeling of shame and disappointment as he'd growl at me and do the job himself - the message: 'You're hopeless!'. It was a one-shot game and if I fluffed it, I'd end up feeling worthless and incompetent and then I'd be sidelined and ignored. This feeling of invisibility to the man I thought was master of the universe created a hunger to be seen and approved of.

As I reflected on this it became clear to me that I had associated criticism of any kind with this feeling of shame, beliefs about being unworthy of attention (a form of love), and with negative judgment. I'd adopted an unspoken belief that criticism was a sign that I was being revealed as an unworthy, incompetent person, and that if someone criticised me it meant they didn't like me, thought poorly of me and (as a natural consequence) didn't want to be with me. My ancestral needs to belong and be connected were in jeopardy.

So there I had it, I understood the pattern. I was in my early 20s at this point. I thought that by understanding it, it might eventually lose its grip on me. It didn't. It lost a little of its overwhelming impact but I was still at the mercy of the Reactions. I got a bit better at hiding its effect, but inside it still hurt the same.

Unfortunately, figuring it out in my head was the easy bit. All it meant is that I knew what kind of demon was outside the window. It didn't change the fact that I was still terrified by it - it still had its reactive grip on me. The neurons that had fired together all those years ago were still wired together.

Neurons that fire together wire together

This might be a good break in the story to say a little more about this 'neurons that fire together wire together' thing. A visual that really helps me with this is a big spider's web with many, many strands connected to many, many other strands. If you ping just one of them, many others move as they are connected to it. In fact to some extent, the whole web feels the vibration.

This is kind of what it's like with our nervous system. Certain neural messages become associated with physiological activity. So the sight of a coiled up scaly thing (Body Sensation through the eyes) gets interpreted as a snake (Perception) and the limbic system in our brain triggers off a bunch of chemicals in our body that put us on red alert because we associate snakes with danger (Reactions).

So in our current story, a Perception of critical speech from someone, certain sensory stimuli (words, tone, facial expressions) are two strands of the web that, when they get pinged, makes me feel an immediate unpleasant Feeling Tone. Through recognising this as criticism, these strands have been linked up with associations (emotional memories) of negativity and criticism, which are linked with feelings of fear of loneliness, worthlessness etc. However the experience just feels like the whole body reverberating from an unpleasant experience. The whole web feels it.

I remember an instance of this in my mid-20s in my first 'real job' in the corporate world - a junior consultant in an HR consulting firm. I was in my boss's office having my first ever performance review. He'd just listed off a whole bunch of things I'd done well and then at the end, described one thing he'd like me to improve. As I walked back to my office I had to intensely direct all of my energy towards desperately holding back tears

Why? Think about it. A middle-aged man with a deep masculine voice (auditory Body Sensations) told me I wasn't good at something

(Perceptions). I had a very strong unpleasant Feeling Tone because of the Reactions that arose (memories of imperfection being linked to feelings of disappointment and worthlessness). I didn't have the skill with Consciousness at the time to see what happened - all I knew was I was really upset and felt ridiculous for it.

Back to the example of my own demon tea party.

For the decade or so around that time, my Davey Jones routine consisted of blame. I could see that Dad had caused these patterns I was struggling with, but they were upsetting and I didn't know how to deal with upset (and frankly, was afraid of it) so I covered it up with blame and criticism towards him.

It took about 10 years for me to realise what the next step was and gather up the courage to take it. This is the hardest bit. You might need some help the first time you do it, especially if there is any chance that it might involve deeply fearful, disturbing or traumatic memories. This step is to walk through the mud puddle so that you know its contours well; to unpack the black bag in the light; to invite your demon in for a tea party.

The problem is, I'd spent so much time fearing it - and I started fearing it at a time when it felt like my very emotional survival was at stake - that there was a lot of fear about inviting that demon in. I didn't know how dangerous it was. What if I let it in and found that it was vicious? What if the mud puddle is really deep? Perhaps the demon could eat me, the black bag could engulf me, the mud puddle could drown me, overwhelm me. I'd most certainly have to experience vulnerability and all of the fear that came with it. And would I survive the tea party? Would I ever come out the other side of the mud puddle, or would I just get stuck in it? If that was the case it might be better never to set foot in it - to just live with the fear, to keep running and blocking.

One of the reasons I fought so hard to keep the demon out was that another of the lessons my father had taught me was that softness and vulnerability were not okay. Indeed, one of the few attributes for which I ever received praise was for being a 'toughie'. Toughness and hardness were good and to be admired. Softness was weak, weak people have no credibility, and people who have no credibility are irrelevant.

That put me in a bind. To face my fears of unworthiness I had to first face my fear of vulnerability, which was strongly linked to my fear of criticism which showed I was unworthy! Aaaaagghhh!!!

Finally, in my early thirties, came a moment of clarity. I found myself having an imaginary conversation with my father for the umpteenth time, letting him know, in very unkind terms how angry I was about the impact he'd had on me. The anger was swirling around and around and the narrative kept fuelling the fire.

Then it hit me how futile this strategy was - this Davey Jones strategy - how I'd been here so many times before and I didn't know how to get out of the rut. It was at that point that I decided that, regardless of my very real fear of facing my own vulnerability, I had to do it. I had to go there.

I had to stop being afraid of myself!

So what does inviting your demon in for a tea party mean? It means facing the fear head on. Feeling it, letting it upset you if that's what it does, naming the hurt that is coursing through your body, letting the emotion have its head. To let out the emotional energy that has been trapped in it (in whatever form it takes) AND to bring the strong light of awareness to the whole experience. This means, in the midst of the experience, putting energy into paying attention: what's going on in the mind? The emotions? The body?

Luckily a friend had been raving about a personal development course she'd done. As it turned out, it was just what I needed. It was all about helping you face your demons; the stuff or your baggage that comes up in your Reactions.

This involved, with the help of others who'd been through it, talking about my difficult experiences and when the emotions came up, letting them. Not cutting them off or trying to bury them but letting the hurt or fear or shame or loneliness just be there and acknowledging it. Naming it and describing it.

For someone who had a visceral fear of my own vulnerable emotions this was terrifying! At first I had thoughts about my parents scoffing at me for doing such a course. The idea of crying in front of other people was itself a source of serious anxiety for me, bringing up all the stuff about judgment for being weak. It was discomfort and unpleasantness on steroids.

However when it was over, I felt an incredible sense of relief. And i wasn't just the temporary relief from having a good cry. It was like the landscape had shifted in a good way. There was a calm and a lightness that was foreign to me. It was lovely. Afterwards I felt incredibly open hearted to everyone I encountered.

As a book-end to this story, the people who ran the course threw out the challenge to everyone there of visiting or calling the person who'd created the pain they were working on that weekend and connecting with them. For everyone I spoke to, that was a parent.

I remember sitting there next to the phone wanting to walk away. I was really afraid of doing it, of possibly being met with more of the stuff that had caused the problem in the first place. I really didn't want to. And to this day I wonder if it was in fact my aversion to weakness that led me to do it.

I think it's the single most courageous thing I've ever done. In the end I picked up the phone and rang the man who'd instilled in me all of these hang-ups and fears of vulnerability, and told him what I'd done that weekend and that I'd forgiven him. We spoke for a couple of hours (which was unheard of). We told each other we loved each other. It's the only time I can remember him telling me that. Our relationship was so much easier from then on. My anger was gone.

This wasn't a total fairy-tale ending. It didn't transform our relationship into one of closeness or deep friendship - that would have required more work and I still had other baggage to work through. But it did allow us to have a good relationship. I really didn't feel like I had a relationship with him at all before as I was aversively holding him at a distance.

Six years later my dad died at just 64 years of age. My mum tells me that phone call was very important. While in some ways it mightn't have been the kindest thing to put myself through, Mum tells me it made an important difference to him. I'm glad I dug deep into my courage that day.

Three important tips about being with strong unpleasantness

Let's look at three very important things to know about facing your fears like this. The first is that there is a difference between facing a difficult emotion with awareness, and indulging it completely.

To face it with awareness means that a little part of you, even in the depths of the fear or hurt, knows that you're just having a tea party with your demon. And while it's scary as hell, it's just a process you're going through, and you will come out of it.

To indulge it completely means you don't have this little part of yourself that knows it's just a process. That can be overwhelming. It can also be counter-productive as you might get too scared and back out. That will possibly increase the fear of the demon.

You might also start making the feelings solid and tangible by turning them into a story that you tell and re-tell and start looking for evidence and sympathy to support a story that keeps you stuck. This could add to, rather than diminish the fear. That's not helpful either.

The second thing to know is that you need to trust your psyche to know how much you're ready for. Don't go inviting demons inside if you're not truly motivated to spend the time and curiosity to get to know them.

For me it was that moment at home alone during the day where I'd just finished that imaginary rant to my father, saying all the things I'd really like to say about how much of a jerk he'd been and how responsible he was for all of my hang-ups and the problems they'd created in my life.

In that moment it hit me just how many times I'd done this; how many hours of my life I'd wasted on imaginary conversations; how much of my emotional energy I'd squandered on anger and keeping these fires burning. I was stuck and in pain! It was then that I decided to do whatever it took to disempower this demon.

For my entire adult life I'd been pretty good at solving my own problems, but I realised I was spinning my wheels and I didn't have my usual sense of possibilities for what to do. This is Mara (the killer) killing our creativity and ensnaring us in a trap. I wanted to drop the anger but I couldn't, and I didn't know how to get out of that rut.

But I had reached a point of no return. I didn't care what monsters I had to face, how scared I had to be. I had to move on. It's that kind of commitment you need if you want to make friends with demons of the very scary variety. It's not to be done casually, but the rewards are enormous, which brings me to the third thing.

The third thing is that there is something truly magic that happens when you face your fears fully. It's like a blanket has been lifted from you, a heaviness is gone. You may feel a real lightness, or maybe just less heaviness. It's pretty likely that those rustling bushes outside the window will scare you less, immediately. In some cases they can even stop scaring you much at all.

Don't go looking for this to happen: it will happen on its own if you have genuinely befriended your demon, if you have truly visited the bottom of your mud puddle, or thoroughly explored your black bag. In fact if you go looking for the pain to stop, you might be tempted to get the tea party over with as quickly as possible, hoping to minimise the pain. Demons can smell this attitude a mile away - they'll head back outside to the bushes under your window and you'll be none the wiser. Remember as long as you're too afraid to be with them, they'll see their job as keeping you alert and on edge. They don't know any better.

Remember that the task is to know the demon really well. It may also be that you'll need to let it back in from time to time if you're finding yourself avoiding it again or being affected by that reactive pattern - the web pinging. However it's never as scary as the first time, and if you commit to facing your unpleasantness as a way of life, you will get to a point where scary is just no longer a word that fits.

Now here's a practical guide to actually doing it. It consists of four simple steps that can be applied in or soon after most situations. I've turned this into a workbook that walks you through the steps in more detail (find it on the Tools page on my website, as listed in the Resources section of this book), but you can try a basic version of it here on a small demon.

Pick a current or recent situation that's been causing you some angst or upset. Not all mud puddles are as scary as each other: you probably have a number of them and they'll vary in the strength of the fear reaction they trigger. On a scale of 1 to 10 where 1 is mildly unpleasant and 10 is overwhelmingly painful, choose a situation that's a two or a three.

Until you're practised at this you might need support for anything with a higher score (see the Resources page), so just choose a mild one to start with. Then do the exercise, giving plenty of time for each step. It's important not to rush the process.

Practical Tip: Four steps to a demon tea party

1. **Relax**

   Find somewhere quiet and comfortable and sit still where you won't be disturbed. Relax the body. If it helps, do a progressive relaxation where you spend a few minutes focusing on each part of your body from the top of your scalp down to your toes, and try to let go of tension and relax each bit. If it helps, find a guided meditation on the internet to take you through this part.

2. **Observe mental activity**

   Bring the situation to mind - the setting, the people, the circumstances, what happened. Bring it back to life in your mind. Now ask yourself: what's going on? What's the story and how is it being told?

- Are there mental movies? If so, what's the plot? Is it a victim movie about poor me (perhaps waiting for a saviour to enter or someone to at least soothe your pain)? An action/revenge movie where you're taking matters into your own hands to 'fix it' somehow? A movie about escape, heartbreak, or a scary movie where there's a danger lurking? Some other kind?

- Is there a mental dialogue or script arising? How would you describe it?

- Is there any commentary or narrative? What is it?

3. **Identify emotions**
   What emotions are present?

   - Where are they on the scale of pleasant to unpleasant?

   - Can you name them? Don't force the answer to this, just ask yourself what's there and wait for answers to arise. If they're not quite right, just ask yourself again and wait. You'll know when you get the right words. There could be more than one, so keep going until you feel that you've recognised all the main ones. (There's a link to a free tool to help with this on the Tools page of my website.)

   - If there's fear present, fully explore it. Explain the fear in detail to yourself as if you know nothing about it. Tell the fear-story fully from beginning to end. If there is more than one fear, you might note them down and then have a separate tea party on each one that you identify. Ask yourself questions about it – get really curious. What's the fear behind the fear?

4. **Observe the body**
   Ask yourself these questions to get in tune with what's going on in your body.

   - Where is there sensation?

   - What are the sensations?

   - Is it moving or still? If it's moving, what kind of movement is it? Is it smooth, jittery, fluctuating? How would you describe it?

- Does it have a temperature?

- Does it have a weight?

- In what way is it unpleasant?

As a short-hand guide through this activity, after relaxing the body–mind, you simply bring the situation into your awareness, explore mind activity, then emotions, then body sensations.

Once you feel a sense of completion with this activity, take a moment to notice your current experience. Is it any different to the experience you were having at the beginning of the exercise? If so, how?

Summary

- The Second Great Task is to dismantle our reactive habits - our Davey Jones and Cookie Monster routines. These are two sides of the same coin.

- The Davey Jones routines are our ways of refusing to be with our experience as it is, of trying to escape from unpleasant feelings by getting rid of them (our fight or flight tendencies) so that we can always have the pleasant.

- Numbing to unpleasant feelings has a cost: to some extent we numb all feelings.

- Dismantling our reactivity requires us to get to know intimately our own reactive patterns (instead of numbing to them). Gotama's Five Clusters of experience (Body Sensations, Feeling Tones, Perceptions, Reactions and Consciousness) are a helpful tool for using our Consciousness to achieve this.

- The Perceptions and Reactions clusters are affected by our beliefs. A great deal of our stress in life comes from faulty beliefs. Lack of worthiness is a common faulty belief in the West, threatening our needs for connection and belonging.

- Gotama highlighted three characteristics of reality that we fail to incorporate into our beliefs and expectations in life. These *Three Tragic Misunderstandings* delude us and generate a great deal of pain.

  Unpleasantness: People and things in life cannot bring us indelible, constant happiness. Everything in life contains the seeds of unpleasantness. Our tragic misunderstanding of this leads us to look to them for more happiness than they can ever give.

Impermanence: Nothing is reliable, stable, or permanent. Our tragic misunderstanding of this leads us to pin our happiness on unstable things and to expect them to be reliable. This includes our favourite displaced divinities (concepts we believe to be ubiquitous, reliable, or to explain everything).

Not-self: Experience occurs to and within our self as it does with every living being. It's not 'my' experience or 'me', it's just human experience flowing. Our tragic misunderstanding of this leads us to create and protect ideas about a fixed identity for our self as if Who I Am is something set and unaffected by conditions, rather than fluid and arising in response to conditions. We co-opt certain parts of our experience into our identity, building them into a concept of Me that we then project and protect.

- There are many methods for having a tea-party with our demons. Anything that helps us know our fears - the mind activity, emotions and body sensations - is helpful. The Flourish Personal Growth website has several resources to help with this including an online course, virtual coaching and community.

- Enlist some support if your demon is very scary, and/or you're not familiar with facing your fears. Therapy can be really helpful for this.

Chapter 8: The Third Great Task

Fully experience non-reactivity

The third key element of Gotama's teachings seems to receive relatively little time and attention in both books and retreats. Perhaps that's because it's a simple concept. That's not to say it's easy to practise, but it's not complex.

Here's the guts of it. When we stop impersonating Davey Jones, that is, feeding our hungers to avoid unpleasantness through reactive habits, their intensity begins to fade. When reactivity ceases what we are left with is something quite beautiful, in fact, spectacular! When we stop fanning the flames of reactivity, when we face our unpleasantness and let go of our Me Brochure, what emerges is an incredible peace and happiness. This is quenching: nirvana.

It's not the type of happiness that comes from getting what we want, from satisfying our hungers. It has a different quality. It's not attached to the arrival of something external. Rather, it's simply what arises when we stop hungering for things to be different; when we stop reacting to the pleasant and unpleasant by craving more or pushing away; when we stop projecting and protecting our Me Brochure. It's a joy-infused and peaceful calm whose potential was there all along. It was the constant reactivity that got in the way.

The suttas offer many descriptors: a state of peace, of purity, and of freedom; sublime and auspicious; wonderful and marvellous; an island;

a shelter and a refuge. However people often confuse this experience of quenching with blissful states of absorption in meditation. Gotama didn't consider these necessary for awakening; indeed many of his followers had awakening experiences without them.

Freedom from reactivity essentially means that we experience life as it is, without fanning the flames of hungering and reacting to them. Through training our minds to see our experience as clearly as we can, the hungering impulses drop away, as does the reactivity that used to follow on their tails. We stop feeling the need to make Me the centre of the universe, and we stop making everything a big deal. The pleasures and displeasures of life are just different experiences in the normal flow of things rather than good or bad things happening to Me.

This makes life much lighter, easier and more joyful. It's much less troublesome. It allows us to open our attention to the moment we're in as it is, rather than as it relates to Me. Open heartedness arises easily, friendliness, warmth, a sense of love for this moment and of empathy for the struggles that are going on around us all the time. There's a freedom and a calm. Our creative capacities are fully available. There's a sense of awe at life and the world and the fact that we are even here at all.

Passion and desire

One of the classic definitions of awakening is the going out of a lamp or fire. The idea is that the heat of lust, passion and desire vanish. In our modern world that idea can often stop people in their tracks. Peace, calm, joy? Yes please. But vanquishing desire and passion? Hang on a minute! Isn't that the beauty of life?

Many of the messages we receive from our modern society put these experiences up on a pedestal as what it's all about. Can you feel the clinging to pleasure as this is challenged, even as you read this?

First, it's important here to distinguish between passion that's felt as creative, or life-embracing energy, and passion that's felt as impulsive, reactive lust or desire. Energy is helpful and indeed moves us along the path. It's a part of being human. If we have no desire for anything, we would never do anything - including meditation or practising the dharma!

However, when we are in the grip of lust or impulsive passion and desire, we have a one-tracked mind, and we lose our grip on reality as it is: our Perception is not clear. If we don't get what we are lusting after, we become very unhappy and can often cause harm as a way of discharging that unpleasant feeling. That hunger is imbued with a desperation which, if you look closely, has an unpleasant Feeling Tone.

Here's a scenario that might ring true for anyone who loves (has a passion for) good coffee, as most Australians do. Imagine you're on holidays in Europe. You've looked on the internet, and your itinerary for the day takes you nowhere near the one cafe that has good coffee ratings.

Can you accept that you won't get a good coffee today and drop the issue? Or do you spend the rest of the day complaining and feeling annoyed at the fact that such a modern place hasn't cottoned on to good coffee yet? That's the difference between passion that's energy, and passion that's reactive desire.

Of course it's easy to think of examples that show how non-trivial passion and desire can be. The courts are full of sexual assault and murder cases where impulsive, reactive desire has resulted in great harm.

But of course this is not the only kind of desire that causes harm. Impulsive desire rips families apart over inheritances, destroys people's health through drugs, alcohol and over-consumption, and leads to mass murder in struggles for political power. It's the kind of desire that moves us to mindless action to quench our passion for something, regardless of the consequences. It's the impulse that says 'I HAVE to have this thing', or 'I'm not okay unless I get this experience', or 'I don't care who I tread on, I'm doing this'.

The spiritual achievement paradox

Practising the dharma does make you happier and calmer and reduces the amount of pain in your life. However there's an irony in what's required to achieve this. To make any meaningful progress on this path, you need to acknowledge the wish for greater ease … and then let it go! Let it fade into the background rather than it taking up the foreground. The reason is, as you may have gathered by now, that an integral part of progressing on this path is accepting and being with unpleasant experiences.

Recently I was watching a fly buzzing incessantly at the window. The window couldn't open but there was an open door on the other side of the room which gave access to the outdoors. Try as I might to encourage the fly away from the window towards the door, it kept returning, obsessed with getting 'out there'. There are many dead flies on windowsills.

The desire for awakening is a bit like this. If we are obsessed with getting somewhere, that is, somewhere other than here, we'll die on the windowsill. That urgency to get out is, in itself, a form of aversion to our current experience. We need to acknowledge that we want to move to a different way of living, then turn our attention to the room we're in and get to know it well. Acknowledge the goal, and then set it aside.

One of my favourite Buddhist authors, Barry Magid, cautions us to be aware of any 'secret practice' we might have developed based on 'curative fantasies' about our life. In his excellent book *Ending the Pursuit of Happiness*, he says of the dharma:

> "It is not a means to an end. It's not a way to become calmer, more confident, or even 'enlightened'. Indeed, our whole practice can be said to be about putting an end to self-improvement, an end to our usual compulsive pursuit of happiness … Not that we can't be happy (or enlightened), it's just that we'll get there by a very different route than we once imagined - and it may not look anything like what we expected when we started out."

Realistically, the reason most people approach the dharma is to deal with (get rid of) some difficulty in their life. I think it's important to be honest about that. It's an appealing idea that if we can just get to the right place, then 'aahhh', we can sit down and rest, trouble free for the rest of our lives.

However awakening isn't a black and white thing. It's not the case that once you experience it, that's it, you're there permanently.

I remember reading about the Buddhist teacher Jack Kornfield who went to Asia and became a Buddhist monk in the 1970s. An accomplished student, full of equanimity and calm he was unsettled to find that when he returned to the familiar surroundings of his home and family, he slipped straight back into old reactive habits. I know this experience – my family of origin is the most challenging environment for my practice. It takes time, practice and exposure to different situations to solidly entrench our new habits of being.

Gotama taught that our experience is the product of conditions that are present internally and externally to us. Experiencing awakening with one set of external conditions present (e.g. living in an Asian Buddhist monastery) doesn't mean that we'll have the same experience in another set of conditions (back home with the old family habits that bring with them old emotional memories).

Of course as we get to know our own body–minds better and learn to manage our minds more skilfully, the internal conditions that we take with us can become more stable and resilient. This is dharma practice - focusing on the process of life, on fully inhabiting it and knowing it, letting go of reactivity, and really inhabiting this wonderful non-reactive state when it's present. The focus of practice is on the process, not the outcome.

Example

I experience this frequently in my sport. In one World Championships I came in ranked number one in the world in my best event, so I definitely wanted to win.

However the 400 m hurdles is a very technical race. There are 10 hurdles around the track, which means 10 opportunities to muck things up. You have to get your stride pattern right in the 35 m between hurdles so that you maintain your momentum and clear them efficiently.

If you have to slow down to clear a hurdle, you then have to accelerate again after it, thus robbing you of precious energy and ruining your time. You can imagine then that a head wind, or getting distracted by another athlete, or misjudging your pace can spell disaster.

To perform well I needed to devote all of my attention to execution. The night before the final I noticed my mind activity had really ramped up and was all over the place. What if I misjudge my pace into the head wind? What if I get distracted by the ex-World Champion who's in the lane next to me? These mental movies were interspersed with scenes of crossing the line first or standing on the podium receiving a gold medal. The energy was a little fearful - the fear of disappointment, of not reaching my goal.

None of this was helpful. I had to re-focus my attention, and I had to do it fast. I'd already competed in the 100 m and the heptathlon and needed to rest! And by 12 o'clock the next day I had to be singularly focused on executing this race.

Thinking about the desired outcome - receiving the gold medal - was not helpful. The only way to achieve it was to stop focusing on it and place my attention on what was in front of me, on what I had to do.

Because of my dharma practice I know what kind of things (conditions) calm my body–mind: meditation, yoga, listening to dharma podcasts. I did those. The body–mind calmed down, and I had a fabulous nine-hour sleep.

I got up the next day with a calm mind, very present to my current experience. I felt nervous but strangely calm at the same time. The mind's energy for charging off to the imaginary finish line or the podium wasn't strong. If I found it going there, it was easy to sweep it back on to executing the race. I did. And I won. It was only by focusing on the process that I could achieve my goal. That's what dharma practice is like.

About 100 years after the Buddha's death, Zhuangzi put this eloquently:

When an archer is shooting for nothing he has all his skill.

If he shoots for a brass buckle he is already nervous.

If he shoots for a prize of gold

he goes blind

or sees two targets

- he is out of his mind!

His skill has not changed.

But the prize divides him.

He cares.

He thinks more of winning than of shooting

and the need to win

drains him of power.

Dharma practice is about the shooting; it's about executing the 400 m hurdles; it's about the process of being alive; it's about our experience of being human, here, now, with whatever is in front of us. It's about attending fully to this moment in the journey. It's about using what we've learned about our own patterns of experience so we can deal with this moment skilfully and mindfully. It's about seeing clearly how our experience works and experimenting for ourselves with Gotama's insights about what causes peaceful, open-hearted flourishing as a human being.

A way of travelling, not a destination

Awakening is a gradual process - a pattern of habits developed over time. You might experience awakening just momentarily or for a period of time, and then you regress because certain conditions arise in your life that test your new habits in ways they're not yet strong enough to withstand. You can go through patches of lively dharma practice and then find your experience falling back into old patterns.

In the Pali canon there are numerous stories where people speaking with Gotama achieve instant awakening after their conversation. However these people had been doing their gradual preparation prior to this. Awakening is the moment where our gradual progress bears fruit. One Buddhist monk and author, Anālayo (p126), describes it like this:

> "The conditions must exist but the time required for such gradual preparation to bear fruit varies greatly according to the individual. ... Most practitioners experience a cyclic succession of progression and regression oscillating within a fairly broad spectrum."

As I mentioned, regular meditation - by itself, even without any insight - often produces greater calm in people's lives. Some research shows that $12\frac{1}{2}$ minutes of meditation is all that you need to reap some of the neuropsychological benefits of meditation; to get a bit of calm. This helps improve the experience of life to an extent: it takes the edge off the stress and reduces our reactivity a little. But it doesn't fundamentally change the experience of life, that is, the way we receive it. It just makes our buzzing at the window a bit less unpleasant.

That's not to say that dedicating a lot of time to meditation can't produce insight. Zen in particular, which focuses on engaging in meditation and rituals with little or no emphasis on studying the dharma, has produced many highly developed individuals. Their idea is to experience not-self directly using, among other things, enquiry questions (*koans*) that have no rational answer, so encouraging the mind to let go of familiar ways of thinking.

In contrast to the common traditional view, if you accept Stephen Batchelor's translation that reactivity arises with unpleasantness (rather than causes it), then if you let go of reactivity, all you're left to deal with is the inevitable unpleasant bits of life. Birth, sickness, old age, death, not getting what we want, getting what we don't want, being separated from what's dear to us and our psycho–physical ways of experiencing the world - they are all part of life and they can involve unpleasantness. We accept and respond to them without fanning the flames of upset. We stop treating unpleasantness as if it were an intruder in our life, but treat it as part of the family.

This changes the experience of it markedly. We still have some unpleasant experiences, but it's not a problem. We stop looking for the silver bullet to transform our lives into pain-free zones, and we accept, expect and get to know the difficult spaces in our lives. This is a process, a true journey, which over time, and bumpy bits, and progression and regression, leads us to awaken in our lives.

Instead of thinking about awakening as a destination, it can be helpful to think of it as a way of travelling. Where the path goes isn't the point. The way you experience travel is where it's at.

And beware of the catch-phrase 'enjoying the journey', because that suggests that the whole trip 'should' be enjoyable if we're practising right. Again, the curative fantasies sneak in - the wish to avoid all unpleasant experiences. I can't imagine that even Gotama enjoyed the demise of his body as he died at age 80 in ancient India. However the physical pain is all that he would have endured. He wouldn't have cooked up a whole batch of distress for himself in his reaction to it.

So if awakening is a way of travelling that depends on conditions, not a permanent destination, then why was Gotama called a Buddha, *an awakened one*? That sounds like a permanent designation.

This points to the important role of our internal conditions. The dharma is something we practise so that it wears itself into our way of receiving life, so that new neurons fire together and wire together. The more that it infuses our lens on the world, the more it becomes the default internal set of conditions, and therefore the more it permeates our experience.

Gregory Kramer gave a fascinating talk about his experience of coming very close to death, arguably a situation that might be seen as the ultimate test of our practice. He was in hospital with cancer and his body reacted badly to some drugs that the doctors had administered.

The key point I remember was that when it comes to a crunch-moment like dying, none of the lists or concepts got a look-in. All that showed up was the extent to which he'd internalised the practices so that they were the default setting for his experience of life.

It's striking how calmly and openly he speaks of an experience which would rock most of us. The practices of acceptance and curiosity were so well entrenched for him that they even showed up in a threatening situation where he was barely conscious.

For me this example demonstrates the idea that even though awakening, like all things, depends on conditions, if we are committed to dharma practice it comes to infuse our internal conditions which we take with us through all external circumstances. That's not to say it can't be reversed, but if dharma practice is your way of living, it becomes increasingly unlikely.

Some descriptive lists

Gotama was renowned for his lists of things. Because he was living in a pre-literate society this was how he helped people remember the teachings. Three of his lists are key to the experience of awakening.

The Four Divine Abodes

First, there are the *Four Divine Abodes* (often called the *Brahma Viharas*, also sometimes referred to as the *Four Immeasurables*). These are characteristics that typify someone with an awakened mind:

- **Warm Friendliness:** (often called loving kindness) refers to a feeling of kindness and good will towards all sentient beings, human and otherwise

- **Compassion:** an understanding, empathy and care towards all others in their moments of suffering, and a desire to help

- **Empathic Joy:** (often called sympathetic joy) refers to a genuine happiness at others' joy or good fortune

- **Equanimity:** a calm emotional balance in the face of both pleasant and unpleasant experiences.

The Seven Factors of Awakening

The factors that help sweep the mind in this direction are the *Seven Factors of Awakening*, which I mentioned earlier. Here they are again:

- Mindfulness/Awareness
- Curiosity (about our experience through the lens of the dharma)
- Energy
- Delight
- Tranquillity
- Mental integration (consistency of mental direction)
- Equanimity

Gotama described these factors as being like rivers flowing to the sea. They incline the mind towards awakening. They're considered to be a sequential process whose outcome, as you can see, is to dwell far more often in one of the four states of the Divine Abodes. Indeed, equanimity is considered to be a 'suitable mental condition for awakening'.

Here's how this works. When we've established a stable state of mindfulness (Mindfulness/Awareness), we get curious about and investigate the nature of our experience. Gotama shared his insights about our experience through the dharma, which we can use as we investigate it directly (Curiosity). Once this investigation gains momentum (Energy), our insight grows and we start to see our experience more clearly. This is inspiring (Delight). If we can avoid the temptation to start craving for this pleasant experience to continue, and the mind doesn't become agitated, continued contemplation leads to a state of calm (Tranquillity) and the mind stops jumping from pillar to post (Concentration). As this process continues and our insight deepens, equanimity becomes a more common experience, and our reactive habits start to fade (Equanimity).

This isn't a to-do list for awakening: it's more of a description of the natural flow of experience that leads to it. Notice the starting point is mindfulness. At least this factor, and the second, Curiosity, we can deliberately cultivate.

The Five Hindrances

In contrast to that list, Gotama presented another list of factors that get in the way of our path to awakening - the *Five Hindrances* to progress on the path. These are considered to impede the establishment of the awakening factors. A mind free from these hindrances is often referred to as *luminous*. Here they are in Table 5, along with some similes Gotama used for them.

Table 5: The Five Hindrances, with similes[2]

Hindrance	Explanation	Simile given by Gotama	Simile for overcoming it
Sensual desire	colours our entire perception	water coloured with dye	relief from a debt
Aversion	our body–mind is agitated and heated	water heated to the boil	recovery from an illness
Sloth and Torpor	our body–mind has become stagnant	water overgrown with algae	freedom from prison
Restlessness and Worry	our body–mind is tossed about	water stirred by the wind	liberated from slavery
Doubt	clarity is obscured	water is dark and muddy	the safe crossing of a dangerous desert

The more awakened our state is, the less we are buffeted around by circumstance. We experience pain and pleasure as they come and go, but we don't get caught up in trying to make the pleasant last longer than it does or the pain vanish faster than it does. We see our self as a dynamic process rather than a fixed identity, and we let experience flow through us without our ego trying to pin down certain parts of it as Me.

The idea that life's pleasures can bring us lasting permanent joy becomes a thing of the past because we know that, by its nature, life contains all sorts of things in all shades of pleasantness and unpleasantness. We accept this and it's not a problem.

The idea that if we can arrange life just so then we'll live happily ever after makes us laugh. We inhabit our present more fully and attentively.

From Anālayo p188–199

Over time the reactivity disappears. There's pleasant stuff, there's unpleasant stuff, and we let it come and go.

The spiritual bypass

Most people come to the dharma out of a desire to let go of some kind of unpleasantness in their life. However there are two important caveats here.

The first is the paradox that in order to release ourselves from the grip of unpleasantness, we need to be prepared to first face it and experience it fully. The dharma does offer a release from a great deal of suffering, but it's not a quick fix. It's through our willingness to be with and know our experience intimately, that we stop being thrown around by it.

Secondly, experiencing awakening doesn't mean that you'll never again experience any shade of unpleasantness. In the traditional view, because all unpleasantness is created by hungering (craving) which we then react to, if we can give up hungering then, Woohoo!!, we get out of the unpleasant bits of the human experience. So if we have a rotting tooth, as long as we give up the aversion to the pain, we can get out of the pain all together.

In contrast, the secular approach sees that unpleasantness still exists (the rotting tooth still hurts) but the extra angst we heap on top of it (which is most of our unpleasantness) can be released.

You can see the appeal of the traditional version - total freedom from unpleasant experiences. However if you look closely, you'll see that offering a complete release from all unpleasantness is, in itself, a kind of aversion to part of the human experience. Ironically, this version is appealing BECAUSE of our aversion to unpleasantness - despite aversion being at the very root of unpleasantness itself.

The term *spiritual bypass* initially referred to the ability to experience bliss states without having faced your own reactive habits, and to conclude from this that you can get away with it. It refers to meditators having what Zen practitioners call a *kensho* experience. Essentially, this is an experience of not-self and then assuming that this means that they've 'made it' and therefore there is no need to look at their own difficult spaces. The logic goes: if I achieved this blissful experience without facing any of my painful stuff, then I can get away without facing it at all. Awakening without the bumpy bits.

For me, the spiritual bypass shows the motivation for dharma practice is to remove all pain from life. This is a stubborn non-acceptance of the fact that unpleasantness is a part of life. This logic goes: if I just meditate enough and study the dharma enough and behave like a good Buddhist, then I get out of all the unpleasantness of being human. Aversion.

People who are out of touch with their emotional world can often be attracted to the spiritual bypass in the mistaken belief that their emotional detachment from life is some kind of spiritual attainment. The Buddha never spoke of detachment in this way. What we need to detach from is the grip of our reactive hooks so that they don't drive our behaviour. Make no mistake, the dharma is about experiencing life fully, not cutting off from it.

You will have gathered by now that awakening takes effort. As discussed in the First and Second Great Tasks, we need to be mindful of our reactive habits and diligent in looking at them, courageous in being with them, and vigilant in monitoring our experience with them.

However the Third Great Task also requires another kind of effort: not just the attentiveness to notice experience of non-reactivity, but also deliberately taking it in, not just letting it pass us by.

The Task: Fully experience non-reactivity

A well-known tendency of the human body–mind is what psychologists call the 'negativity bias'. This is the tendency to over-attend to the negative and under-attend to the positive. In Rick Hanson's book *The Buddha's Brain*, he describes our minds as being 'Teflon for the positive and Velcro for the negative'. Our brains notice, store and retrieve negative information more quickly and reliably than they do positive information.

In addition, we have the negative eddy. If we've just had a negative experience (one that has fear hormones and neuro-chemicals coursing through our body) we are more likely to interpret the next circumstance we encounter as negative. The negative eddy sucks anything nearby into its downward spiral.

It makes sense that we evolved this way. When we lived under the law of the jungle, if we were going to make an error of judgment, it was far better to make an overly negative judgment (e.g. I thought there was a tiger in the bushes but there isn't) than it was to make an overly positive one (e.g. I didn't think there was a tiger in the bushes, but there … gulp!).

It also makes sense that if there has been danger nearby, we stay on high alert for more danger. It's a self-protective mechanism that has our mind looking for sources of danger because of this high-alert state. However, once again, in our modern societies, we no longer live under the law of the jungle. Our societies have progressed faster than our genetic tendencies.

The Third Great Task is to fully experience non-reactivity; to viscerally inhabit the spectacular experience of nirvana that arises from it. This challenges us to notice the experience of non-reactivity when we have it. Knowing what we know about the negativity bias, this is no mean feat. It challenges us to stop and really take notice of positive experiences; to undermine our Teflon-for-the-good tendencies.

You've probably experienced non-reactivity. It might only be momentary or maybe longer. I remember driving to my meditation group one night. I was just turning out of my street when I noticed how deeply happy I felt for no apparent reason. There was a sense of not wishing, wanting, or looking for anything, of being completely happy to be right where I was doing what I was doing.

I remember another one when I was doing the dishes, just looking out at the afternoon sun on the trees. There was nothing remarkable about my circumstances. However the feeling imbued my whole body and mind. It was joyous but calm, like I was bathing in a warm joy.

So how do we undermine our Teflon tendencies? Hanson has a whole book on this called *Hardwiring Happiness*. Essentially, notice the details, linger on them, drink them in physically, and share them. Turn positive experiences into visceral ones that we feel in our bodies by attending to, maybe sharing, feeling and savouring the details of them. Bring them alive in our body–mind, infuse our physical body with them, so that they are felt strongly and are easy to remember and recognise.

It's also helpful to notice the conditions that bring this experience about. Because we're Velcro-for-the-bad, I'd recommend dialling down the unnecessary negative stimulation of your body–mind. One prime example is watching or reading the news, which I call the Crime, Death and Destruction Report. There are other ways to stay in touch with society that are nowhere near as biased towards generating fear.

I've been using *The Conversation*, a website which has experts writing on topics of the day. Other websites, such as *Yes!* and *Greater Good* offer a diet of positive and constructive articles. I'd highly recommend unhooking from the Crime, Death and Destruction report and finding other, more balanced media to consume. Because of our negativity bias, if we want to see the world in a realistic way, we actually need to bias ourselves towards the positive.

Fortunately, the negative is not the only thing that snowballs in our body–mind. In my experience, we are also naturally inclined to the positive, recognising it as good for us. However we need to cultivate the habit of registering deeply the positive experiences in our lives so that our body–minds know which way to turn.

Practical tips

A practical suggestion on this front is to keep a gratitude diary. There's now a lot of research on gratitude and it's emerged as a very powerful practice. Keeping a gratitude diary simply involves leaving a notebook next to your bed and each night, before you go to sleep, writing down three things for which you feel grateful, based on your experience of that day.

It's important to understand that this is different from just listing three 'good things'. Gratitude is not just liking something; it's appreciation for something you don't control. It acknowledges that you've been the beneficiary of good fortune.

So for example, 'I'm grateful that I've got a nice clean house today' doesn't cut it if you are the one who cleaned the house. You controlled that. However coming home and finding that your partner cleaned the house unprompted could inspire gratitude, or feeling grateful that you have enough money to pay a cleaner to clean your house (that's at least partly good fortune).

Of course on some days it can be difficult to find the feeling of gratitude, but it's important to persist. On these days it might be something as small as being grateful for the sunny day, or for being lucky enough to live in a safe country where you can walk home from the bus without feeling afraid, or getting over a cold quickly, or the friendliness of your barista, or having a healthy child or pet. It's important that the gratitude is genuine though: you don't want to list things that you 'should' be grateful for if you don't feel it. Keep it real!

Another tip is to share experiences of non-reactivity with others when you have them. Describe them in as much detail as you can.

And a third suggestion is to use journaling to help you pay attention and describe any moments or longer where you experience the things described here.

Summary

- The Third Great Task is to fully inhabit non-reactivity: the quenching of the fires of greed, aversion and confusion and the wonderful experience that arises from this; nirvana. This means to notice the experience and take it in.

- Like all things, awakening is the product of certain conditions coming together. Dharma practice is about cultivating the internal conditions (primarily our own minds) for this freedom from reactivity. Therefore, like all states, it's not necessarily permanent. We can have fleeting experiences of awakening (or longer) in our everyday life. However with continued committed practice, the dharma wears its way in to our default way of receiving life, which makes regression less likely.

- People sometimes mistake blissful meditation states for nirvana. Gotama was clear that these states were not necessary for awakening. Indeed it's possible to become attached to the pleasure of these states (and with attachment comes reactivity, like getting grumpy that I didn't get my meditation today).

- Detachment from experience or emotion is another experience sometimes mistaken for awakening. Non-reactivity comes from non-attachment, that is, not desperately chasing pleasant experiences and running from unpleasant ones. Where Gotama used words that can be translated as 'detachment' they do not refer to disengaging or cutting off from life, but rather, from the grip of our reactive hooks.

- Gotama gave some descriptions of the awakened experience via some of his lists. These include the Four Divine Abodes (universal friendliness, compassion, empathic joy, equanimity) and the Seven Factors of Awakening (awareness, curiosity, energy, delight, tranquillity, mental integration, equanimity). Also relevant is the contrasting list of the Five Hindrances which can knock us off the path to awakening (sensual desire, aversion, sloth and torpor, worry, doubt).

- The negativity bias in our DNA means we need to over-attend to the positive so that it doesn't slide off like Teflon. This means we need to be deliberate in feeding our mind more positivity (even just to have a realistic perception of the world) and specifically in noticing and fully inhabiting the experience of non-reactivity when it's present.

- A gratitude diary is a powerful way to build the habit of noticing the positive. Finding more balanced sources of information than the news is also helpful, as is journaling and sharing in detail, any experiences of non-reactivity and the states that arise from it.

Chapter 9: The Fourth Great Task

Walk the path

The first three Great Tasks are mostly about our inner world. They are about what we attend to and our internal reactions or responses to things. The Fourth Great Task brings together both our internal and external worlds. It's a bit like a checklist for bringing Gotama's insights to life. This last Great Task is called the *Eightfold Path*.

The Eightfold Path covers three areas: Wisdom, Conduct (often termed ethics), and Attentiveness (often termed consciousness or awareness). They're traditionally translated with the word 'Right' at the start of each fold. However there's compelling evidence that this word wasn't in the earliest recorded versions of the teachings, but was added later. According to Stephen Batchelor, a better translation is the word 'complete' but, as I don't find this helps me understand them, I use them without an adjective. In the secular list below, you can think of each area of focus as describing an approach that's appropriate for practising Gotama's teachings.

Table 6: Secular and traditional labels for the Eightfold Path

Secular	Traditional
WISDOM	WISDOM
View	Right view
Intention	Right thought
CONDUCT	ETHICS
Action	Right action
Speech	Right speech
Livelihood	Right livelihood
ATTENTIVENESS	AWARENESS
Effort	Right effort
Mindfulness	Right mindfulness
Mental Integration	Right concentration

The main reason for me removing the word 'right' from the labels is that it helps avoid falling into the polemical right/wrong, good/bad, should/shouldn't way of thinking. Remember, this is not a list of commandments that result in damnation or salvation. It's a way of understanding our experience and letting go of our mess-making. Gotama gave us this guidance to help us do just that - and the idea is to get out and test this fully in your own life, not to adopt any of it as rightness.

The eight *folds* serve as the architecture for training in many religious traditions. From a secular perspective, they can serve as a guide for looking at the way we live and identifying where we're on or off the dharma track.

In teaching these eight folds, I often find that people are enthusiastic about the focus on practical application … at first. That enthusiasm tends to remain while they learn some specific things to focus on to improve the way they currently do things. For example, tuning in to our intentions before we do things, using some guidelines that help us speak more helpfully, or adjusting our effort away from too much or too little.

As you read through these eight folds however, treat this activity as practice in itself. You'll probably find some of Gotama's suggestions are already in line with the way you live. Some might require small or medium-sized tweaks to your current behaviour, and others would entail quite a shift from some of the ways you currently live: there's quite a gap between what Gotama suggests and the way you currently live your life.

Often, when we get to these parts of the path, we feel deeply uncomfortable. So instead of opening our minds to it, exploring our own reactions with gentleness and curiosity, we fly into reactive mode and try to somehow get rid of the idea.

Among Westerners, contemplating the Eightfold Path can challenge three common impulses. One is the need to be a success. We're going through the areas of life that are helpful to living the path, tick, tick, tick, I'm 'doing well' so far, then - oh no, I'm way off on this one! All of a sudden I feel like I'm failing!

I might try to find a way to minimise the importance of that one, to justify giving it a miss, or maybe ignoring it all together. The worst response is to give up because of it. I say 'worst' simply because it means missing out on the benefit of the dharma: it's not a judgment on the person giving up.

The second impulse is the need for autonomy, which is very strong in Western societies. The Eightfold Path is not a list of commandments. It's not a set of criteria against which you are going to be judged. There are no 'shoulds', 'oughts', 'thou shalts' or 'have-tos' here.

Yet even when I preface talks on the Eightfold Path this way, I find that when we get into them, the fear of these shoulds sneaks in. We can feel like we're being told how to be a good boy or girl by a parent or authority figure, so when we don't measure up, we can get hot under the collar.

A third impulse can also come into play here, not necessarily more prevalent in the West. That is the tendency to 'self', to build that identity for ourselves that we treat as real and solid. If we find too many of the boxes that we can't tick, we can retreat into an identity of a non-Buddhist. That is, something along the lines of 'Well, that's ok for the Buddhists, but I'm not a Buddhist, so I'll leave that one'. The Eightfold Path is about human life. It's about looking honestly at our choices and their consequences, even the ones that we take for granted or have grown up with, or like a lot.

When one of these triggers kicks in, what follows is often one of two methods to try and get rid of the unpleasant feelings (recognise that habit?). Rather than practise the dharma in that moment by seeing and accepting the unpleasant feelings that arise, getting to know them and holding our seat with them, we try to find ways to get rid of them: reactivity in action!

One of the common ways we avoid unpleasant feelings is by rationalising our current behaviour. That way we avoid the discomfort of changing it and avoid feeling uncomfortable about what we're doing now. We might start to make excuses or find arguments as to why this suggestion isn't always a good idea in every circumstance, or how it's not relevant in the modern world. Or 'Everyone I know does this, how could I be expected not to?' These are all attempts to avoid the unpleasant - reactivity.

Another reaction we can have is to judge ourselves. For example, 'I could never give up gossiping about others (one of the elements of Helpful Speech), so I can't do this dharma stuff'. Instead of being willing to look closely and test the idea out for myself, I give up wrestling with it so that I don't have to feel bad about my current life choices or habits.

If these or any other triggers come up for you as you read through the following list, see if you can bring awareness, curiosity and gentleness to it. Don't get annoyed or judge-ey at yourself for having the reaction, but don't indulge it either. Notice the mind activity that arises, the emotions, and the body sensations, and try to just sit with them so that you can get to know them. Invite them in for a tea party and sit at the table with them. If it helps, come back and read this passage:

> There are no shoulds, oughts, or musts.
> Just clear awareness of our choices
> And their consequences.

The Task: Walk the path

The practical challenge with the Eightfold Path is to live it. Here's a simple summary of each fold, along with some questions for reflection.

WISDOM

The first group of folds is made up of everything we've already covered in the first three tasks, plus taking care with our intentions.

View

How do we understand reality? Do we see clearly the pervasive reality of Dependent Arising: the fact that everything arises depending on the presence of causes and conditions? This is the fact that life and everything in this world exists only because the conditions are right for it. Three key implications of this which we've covered previously (the Three Tragic Misunderstandings) are:

- Unsatisfactoriness: Because everything is always changing because of conditions and causes, pinning our hopes on any worldly pleasure as a source of reliable, stable happiness is fool hardy.

- Instability/unreliability/impermanence: Everything is always changing, in a state of flux. Nothing is permanent or always reliable because conditions are always changing – anything can happen any time.

- Not-self: There is no fixed, independent, enduring Me identity that exists and consistently behaves in line with my Me Brochure. 'I' am a dynamic process not a fixed entity. Experience is a process I engage with, it's not something that's 'mine' or 'Me'.

In short, this fold is about seeing clearly the way experience works, à la the First Great Task.

Questions and suggestions

- On what do you pin your hopes for happiness in life? Is it success of some kind, being universally loved, respected, admired, or recognised, having particular possessions? Do these things deliver 100% of the time? What happens for you when they don't?

  - Appreciating the reality that all pleasures pass leads us to stop expecting one thing or another in the world to make us indelibly, enduringly happy. We enjoy them for what they are, but we don't expect more from them than they can deliver.

- How do you react when things change: when you lose a job, friend, partner, money, body function, or other cherished aspect of your life? Is there disbelief? Shock? Denial?

  - To the extent that we have incorporated the reality of ever-present change into our view of life, we are less perturbed when we encounter it. There's less splash and spray when unpleasantness enters the pool of our body–mind.

- How much energy do you put into portraying yourself in a particular way? What is in your Me Brochure? How do you react when someone treats you or speaks of you in a way that is not consistent with this list of descriptors?

  ○ To the extent that we see our self as a process dependent on conditions at any time, we are more comfortable and honest with the various and often inconsistent ways we respond to things. We then spend less time and energy defending a set image of ourselves and glossing over the truth of our experience.

Intention

Sometimes referred to as resolve, Intention is the genesis of our actions. The practice is aimed at cultivating these attitudes until they are our default motives. Gotama advised three Intentions:

- Renunciation

- Freedom from ill-will

- Harmlessness.

Renunciation: Think of this as the determination to see for yourself the nature of worldly pleasures and the type of happiness they bring. It's not about denial or aversion to pleasure, but the clear-minded appreciation of its transitory nature.

In doing this we stop expecting things and people out there to make us happy in any kind of enduring way, and so release our grip on the desperate clinging to them. This belief and expectation become such a habitual way of looking at things that they become part of our Reactions.

This is not about denying ourselves the pleasures in life. It's about our relationship to those pleasures. The task is to be able to experience them and enjoy them without being enchanted by them and putting them in pride of place as the meaning of existence. Look up the definition of 'enchantment' and you'll find something like this:

- to subject to magical influence; to bewitch

- to delight to a high degree

- to impart a magical quality or effect to.

Renunciation is simply about experiencing pleasures just as they are and letting them go on their way, just as they do. It's about enjoying the pleasures but not putting them up on a pedestal and making them the goal of all our energies. It's about seeing through the magical enchantment that says 'Add this thing to your life and you will be happy'.

Freedom from ill-will: This one is most relevant when others behave in unkind ways to us, when a very natural defensiveness arises. We might experience a desire to get revenge or 'Show them they can't treat me like that'.

Sometimes even when we reasonably seek justice, ill-will can slip in the door unnoticed. While this doesn't mean we shouldn't seek justice, the point is to be aware of the attitude or agenda behind it. It doesn't mean we allow others to be unkind or fail to protect ourselves or others from harm. But we grow the attitude of this coming from a desire to protect, rather than the desire to harm the other person in return.

Harmlessness: Harmlessness is a big one; it runs through the other two. Indeed it runs through all of the dharma. It's relevant to many things, from the attitudes we bring to conflicts with our loved ones (and not-so-loved ones), to the thought we put in to what we eat and buy, to the way we self-righteously treat beings that our species decides to designate as a 'pest'. This also extends to our attitude to the environment and the extent to which we want to leave a small footprint from our lives.

There is a subtle but important difference between not carrying an intention of harm, and carrying an intention of harmlessness. Carrying an intention of harmlessness is more active, more responsible. For example, we might say something to a friend, who then has a strange non-verbal reaction. We didn't mean to upset them (we didn't intend to harm), so we don't see a need to ask about the impact it had and express our sorrow at that. We see it as their issue, not ours.

However if we carry the intent of non-harm, our friend's upset matters. We had an effect, even though it was unintentional. The impact matters, so of course we would want to ask about it and to make amends, to reconnect with our friend. There's no need to beat ourselves up for it but, regardless, we want to undo any harm that came from it. Can you hear the more active, responsible attitude there?

This difference is even clearer when it comes to harming non-human beings. Once, when my parents were going away for two days, they accidentally locked their dog inside the house on their farm. Because they didn't know he was inside, they didn't leave him any water. They had a composting toilet, so he couldn't even drink from there! They got home to a very thirsty, very distressed dog.

They didn't mean to distress him, that is, they didn't have an attitude of harm. But if they were more practised in the attitude of non-harm towards animals, they would have made it a priority to make sure he was okay and well looked after before they left.

Lots of people love dogs, so there's a good chance you'll feel the importance of the non-harm attitude with that story. But what about creatures that we don't find cute? What about creatures that we perceive as pests? For example, what if you have more cockroaches in your kitchen than you are happy with? How does the attitude of non-harm apply here?

Here's a hint: pesticides are harmful to cockroaches. Feeling uncomfortable yet? See if you can hold your seat with this. Stick with it, and just notice what comes up for you. Are there excuses arising? Are there some carve-outs to dharma practice being drafted in your mind? Okay, humans yes, but anything I perceive as ugly or with more than four legs, no. Is the desire for convenience and ease arising with vigour?

I had this exact situation in my house. The intent of non-harm towards animals is a strong part of my practice. I searched for 'ethical ways to get rid of cockroaches' and found several articles claiming that they don't like the plant catnip. I thought it was worth a try, so I bought some and grew it (it's super easy to grow!). I put some catnip leaves in the places I most wanted to be cockroach free: the cutlery drawer, the crockery cupboards, the pantry, the tops of the dishwasher drawers.

It worked! The sight of cockroaches is now a rare thing in my house (we've also had many visits from our next-door neighbour's cat!). When we take seriously an intention not to harm, we take active responsibility to find ways around it. If this is a big shift for you, there's no need to be overwhelmed. Just start somewhere with one small change and notice how it feels to make this choice instead of a more harmful one.

Of course, it's impossible to live life and avoid harming any people or creatures ever. Simply walking from the car to the front door probably kills a number of creatures (ants), harvesting vegetables does the same, driving a car, flying on planes, and consuming anything with plastic packaging all contribute harm to the environment. It's impossible to live our lives and completely avoid harm.

But remember, this is not a commandment that will lead to your damnation if you don't follow it perfectly. It's a principle that will lead to a more flourishing life, if you genuinely follow it in whatever ways you can.

Even the ants on the garden path are pretty easy to avoid with just a little attention. In fact they perceive vibration as danger, so if you have ants anywhere you don't want them, tap the area for a while with something that causes the surface to vibrate, and watch as they go about telling each other it's time to leave! (It's actually quite fascinating.) Try it and see for yourself.

Gotama emphasised the importance of bringing mindfulness to our Intentions both before, during and after we act. Essentially, we need to ask ourselves whether the Intention is harmful to ourselves or to others or both.

I mentioned earlier the idea of ceasing to watch the Crime, Death and Destruction Report (the news). The vast majority of the coverage in these programs are show-casing reactivity - addiction to sensory pleasure, ill will and harm. It's very easy for our body–mind to come to the conclusion that this is normal and so not even notice when these intentions arise in ourselves.

Be careful what you compare your life to. Our minds take the shape of what we rest them on.

Sometimes we can do seemingly kind acts but our intention is not kindness. For example, some people have a Cookie Monster routine that involves desperately pleasing others all the time. They can do things that appear kind on the outside, but that come from an intention to ingratiate themselves to others. The intention can be to quell their fear of disconnection. Deep down the intention is kindness to themselves, which is a good thing, but there are better ways to be self-compassionate in this instance.

In other cases, people might do a seemingly kind act so that the recipient 'owes them one'. The intention is to have an investment pay off down the track. That's different to kindness: it's a transaction.

In a similar way, seemingly unkind acts can be driven from a kind intent. For example refusing to give children things they want in order to teach them important lessons for their wellbeing. Or putting an untreatable injured animal out of its agony. Or giving some feedback to a friend who's deluding themselves about something important that is causing harm to themselves and others. These might not please the other person at the time, but they are done from an intention of kindness.

As you start to play with this, there will be times when you decide in the moment, to act in a way that you know causes harm. In these moments, mindfulness after the act is important. Reflect on how it felt. How do you feel about it now? Reflect on the conditions that led you to go down that path. Changing patterns of behaviour takes effort - perhaps you were tired or emotionally drained. Maybe you had to 'not think about it' so that you could make the easy habitual decision. Get curious about how the process of harmful behaviour works.

Don't judge, explore!

The key question is what was the agenda behind the action? What was the result you were hoping to bring about? What result DID you bring about and how does that feel? And to what extent does the Intention to do no harm feature in the answer?

Questions and suggestions

- Next time you have to make a decision about something, tune into your body and ask yourself 'what's there?' The intentions of hoarding pleasure, or inflicting harm of some kind feel very different in the body from open-handedness with pleasure, good will and harmlessness.

    ○ Teach yourself to know the difference. Your body is a very reliable indicator.

- When you identify pleasure addiction, ill will or harmfulness as intentions, see if you can accept and respond to it, rather than resist and react to it.

    ○ Rather than resist the fact that you've found this, and try to justify it, judge it or bend the truth about it, can you bring gentleness, compassion, and curiosity to the process? Can you gently put the judging mind to the side (kindly) and explore the causes and conditions that are at play?

- If you find unhelpful intentions are present, get curious about the process.

    ○ What are the Perceptions at work? What are the Reactions? Any mental movies playing? Narratives? What are the themes? Identify as much of the contents of the Five Clusters as you can.

- Pick one area where your current choices inflict some harm List down what other choices are available. Engage one of the alternatives and notice how it feels when you do it. Where you continue to make harmful choices, bring to mind the detail of the harm they are causing when you make them. Take notice of how that feels in the body.

CONDUCT

This group of three folds is about the ethics of the way we conduct ourselves in day-to-day life. It's often translated as ethics but *Conduct* is also accurate. I prefer the active tone of this translation that focuses me on my personal responsibility for my choices.

Speech

What comes out of our mouths is very important to our path. I remember reading an excerpt from a Baha'i book that went something like this:

Material fire consumes the body.

The fire of the tongue consumes the heart and soul.

Metaphysical arguments about the existence of a soul aside (we know that's not helpful), this is pointing to the harm that can be done with words. (There's that issue of harmfulness again.) So it's not surprising that this part of our life is called out by Gotama.

In essence, he pointed to four aspects of speech. Here's the goal and the non-goal:

Table 7: Characteristics of speech

Speech that's appropriate to the path	Speech that's not appropriate to the path
True	False
Unifying	Divisive
Pleasant/affectionate/endearing	Harsh
Factual, related to the dharma and the path	Idle chatter

Speech that's appropriate to the path	Speech that's not appropriate to the path
Timed well for the receiver	Timed poorly for the receiver
Beneficial	Unbeneficial
Comes from an intent of good will	Comes from an intent of ill will

My short-hand for this list is:

Is it true?

Is it helpful?

Is it the right time?

When I need a quick anchor, the criterion 'helpful' tends to cover all the characteristics other than true and well timed. However I do think it's important to know the full list to ensure that 'helpful' is not helpful to a cause of malice or reinforcing gossip by, for example, 'helping' to fill in the details of a gossip story. Remember, too, that helpful includes the wellbeing of others (divisive or unifying?) as well as the individual you're talking to.

I've had a very interesting journey with this fold of the path. As I entered adulthood, I could honestly claim a pretty good track record on the True criterion. However, the Helpful and Right Time boxes remained empty a lot of the time. I was a bit renowned for my between-your-eyes feedback. I've found these criteria to be extremely helpful with shifting these habits.

Gotama offers some more specifics about the principles for speech that help sweep us onto the path:

Truth: We don't consciously tell a lie for our benefit or someone else's, we are honest if we don't know something. We are 'firm, reliable, no deceiver of the world'.

Unifying: We don't gossip about others in order to divide people or damage relationships, rather, we delight in people getting along.

Harsh: We're not abusive, we use words that are pleasing to the receiver and are affectionate, that are touching, polite and appealing.

Idle chatter: Instead of wasting time and energy on superficial or small talk, and trying to amuse and impress, we shift towards more meaningful communication. When you meet a friend, for instance, maybe ask a question that shows a genuine interest in what's alive for them at the moment. Perhaps something like, 'What's been the highlight of your last week?' Or if your friend wouldn't find it too weird, 'What's most alive for you at the moment?'

The only variation that Gotama indicated he thought was okay was if the words were factual, true and beneficial, but unendearing and disagreeable to others. In this case he suggested taking care with our timing for saying them. In other words sometimes it's okay to tell people things they don't want to hear, as long as they're true, helpful, and timed well.

The last of these criteria, idle chatter, could be the most difficult if you're not used to paying attention to your speech. I have in fact found that I spend much less time on surface chit-chat these days and have even lost my love of large parties because that's the main form of dialogue on offer.

But again, this is not a commandment. Start paying attention to the experience of speaking. When we are exaggerating, embellishing or outright lying, what is that experience like … really? What about when we're gossiping, or even just entertaining? What can you notice about the process, before, during and after these acts?

And then what about using a harsh, stern or aggressive tone, or speech designed to diminish another person? Rather than bringing judgment and shame on yourself for doing these things, can you get curious about it? What was the intent? How did it feel when you did it? What did you notice in the other person? How do you feel now about the impact you had?

Appropriate speech is actually more than just what we say and how we say it. It's about how we communicate, by text, by email, by voicemail, by emoji! And it's also about how we listen. Do we genuinely listen to connect with another's experience? Or do we just shut up for long enough to earn the right to speak again? Do we talk over the top of others? This essentially says to them that we aren't interested in hearing what they have to say. That can be hurtful. It's not really connecting with them.

As I've worked on this over the years (and I still have room for improvement), I've actually found that I enjoy saying less. It's not actually that difficult as there seems to be an endless supply of people who want to do the talking. People also respond well if you're willing to listen. It's a great way to feel connected with people.

Once again, the challenge here is to bring mindfulness to our speech, both before, during and after it as well as the speech that goes on inside our heads: our self talk as psychologists call it. This is the voice that narrates our life and is the script of our mental movies. It's the speech we practise and rehearse, and it shapes our body–mind. It's important to cover that speech base as well.

The Buddhist teacher who ran that first retreat I attended has an entire process that treats dialogue as a meditation. That teacher is Gregory Kramer and his practice is called 'Insight Dialogue'. Gregory is the teacher I referred to in the Introduction as the one who impressed me with the way he embodied what he taught. I highly recommend his books and retreats. In summary the process consists of five aspects:

1. **Pause:** Take a moment to step out of the automatic habits of speech and bring awareness to what's present now in your body-mind, whether those things are pleasant or not. Slow down and allow some space in your experience and your interaction. Don't just bowl headlong into reactive speech, take a moment and ascertain whether what you are about to say really needs to be said.

2. **Relax:** accept your current experience just as it is – whatever's going on. To the extent that you can, relax the body and any reactivity around needs, e.g. to be liked, to be seen, to entertain. Just accept whatever's here and allow it to be here.

3. **Open:** extend the awareness and acceptance of this moment to those you're with.

4. **Trust Emergence:** Don't force dialogue or go looking for things to say; trust that whatever needs to come up will come up between you. Let go of any impulses to control the dialogue or have it go a certain way, just allow it to unfold[3].

5. **Listen Deeply, Speak the Truth:** Listen with your eyes and ears for the heart of the message, and speak truthfully from an authentic place.

Questions and suggestions

- Try to notice when you are speaking compulsively, that is, with a need to be heard. Look at this process closely. What are the

3. Note: He's since changed the title of this one but I prefer this original version.

elements in the Reactions cluster here? What would happen if you didn't speak at these times? Try it out for yourself and observe closely.

- Try Gregory's first instruction: to pause before speaking. It might only be for a second or two at first but see if you can just slow down and notice the intention driving what you're about to say.

- When you feel a conflict arising, and you think you might be reactive, act like a block of wood for a few seconds (i.e. sit there and do nothing) and try to bring mindfulness to what's going on for you. See if you can speak up for that in a way that doesn't blame the other person.

- Identify the idle chatter that you spend the most time on, or the person that you engage in it with the most. See if you can go for a week without doing it. Notice carefully what that's like.

- Look at Table 7 and identify which unhelpful characteristic is most common in your speech. Resolve to improve your track record on it. Let a trusted friend (whom you see frequently) know what you're doing and give them permission to draw your attention to it if you fall off the wagon.

- If you struggle with making your points in a pleasant/endearing way, do a workshop or course to build your constructive communication or conflict resolution skills. Non-Violent Communication (NVC) is a great example of this skill set.

- Read Gregory Kramer's book *Meditating Together, Speaking from Silence*.

- Attend an Insight Dialogue workshop or retreat.

Action

Gotama identified three core parts to Action; he described them as living the path:

1. Not killing (or stated positively, practising universal friendliness toward all beings)

2. Not taking what's not freely given (only taking what's freely given)

3. Not engaging in harmful sexual activity (practising contentment).

These three plus two others tend to be used in Buddhist retreats as the Five Precepts or principles that people agree to on the retreat. The two extras are not lying (covered above under speech) and not clouding the mind with intoxicants.

Practising compassion for all beings; not killing

In some ways this one's pretty straightforward. Clearly, killing living beings is harmful. Gotama advised 'living with our rod laid down, our knife laid down, scrupulous, merciful, concerned for the welfare of all living beings'.

This is one practice where I've noticed people can get reactive, so try and pay close attention to your own experience as you read this section.

While most of us wouldn't think of killing another person, the issue that often comes up here is that of eating meat. The food on Buddhist retreats is almost always vegetarian for this reason. There's no way around it, eating meat is at odds with the idea of not killing. We don't get off the hook just because we pay someone else to do the killing.

People who reactively cling to this pleasure often point to the Dalai Lama who eats meat and use that as a reason to continue doing so. As food is a pleasure that we can be particularly attached to, this is a sticking point for many. Discussions can sometimes get heated on this topic. Many of us have some agitated reactivity arise around it, so if that's happening really try to hold your seat with this one.

When you start to look closely at your consumer choices, you realise what a responsibility we have as we spend our money. We begin to see that we have many opportunities to create demand for compassionate production, including:

- refusing to buy leather goods

- abstaining from dairy foods (To keep dairy cows lactating producers keep them pregnant - the calves are whisked away in the first few days of their lives to be killed for 'veal' often not being fed or looked after in the process.)

- choosing cosmetics and skin care that are officially 'cruelty free'. This is different from signs saying 'not tested on animals'. Many people don't know that many of the big cosmetic and skin care brands still engage in cruel animal testing, or outsource it to a third party (so that they can say they don't test on animals). Or they test the ingredients on animals but not the end product so that they can say the product was not tested on animals.

- not eating animal flesh

- if eating animal flesh choosing brands that minimise the harm they do (e.g. sustainable and ethical fishing, minimising by-catch, ethical farms)

- not eating eggs unless you raise your own chickens including roosters (even buying your own chickens involves killing half of the population of chicks - the male half).

CERTIFIED CRUELTY-FREE BUNNY LOGOS

CHOOSE CRUELTY FREE (CCF)

LEAPING BUNNY

BEAUTY WITHOUT BUNNIES

bunny logos you can trust!

The dharma is a set of insights, principles and guides to be experimented with and tested out fully, not a set of rules, judgments, shoulds or commandments. Just as you won't immediately score 10 out of 10 on the speech criteria, the food and consumer goods issue might be one on which you're starting behind the eight ball.

No problem. There's no lightning bolt that's going to strike you from above. The dharma is a set of ethics, not a prescriptive moral code like The Ten Commandments. It's a set of primary values that can't be reduced to thou-shalts and thou-shalt-nots: we constantly find ourselves in situations where principles conflict with each other.

Gotama did allow his followers to eat meat if that's all they were offered on their alms rounds. Gotama and his followers were essentially beggars. They offered their teachings to anyone who wanted them, and in return, received material support from the communities they interacted with. This included food.

Each day they would take their food bowls and walk the streets in the hope that they would be filled (this was the alms round). Their very survival depended on whatever food they were offered. It made sense that these beggars quite literally couldn't be choosers, out of bare necessity. The exception was if an animal was killed specifically for Gotama or his followers, in which case, they were not to accept the offering.

In dharma practice, we need to exercise judgment as we try to live the principles, based on the situation at hand and the consequences we foresee of our actions.

As with all of the folds in the path, the task here is to look closely at our choices and their consequences, to bring mindfulness to the way we live, to see what leads to flourishing and what doesn't. So get rid of any shoulds about it and get mindful. Email your favourite cosmetics brands and ask them specifically about the three types of testing I mentioned. If you find yourself avoiding that, look closely at what is causing that aversion.

Another idea is to spend some time on the internet finding out how livestock are treated and slaughtered. Perhaps visit a slaughterhouse and ask if you can see it for yourself. If the idea of this repulses you, or you've thought about that for a nano-second then shelved the idea, that's probably something worth looking at more closely. What's the resistance to it? Is there a reactivity around the pleasure of eating meat? Are there beliefs about the impact on your life if you were to eat differently? Mindfully explore these things and see what happens.

One of the beliefs I had (in my perception of vegetarianism) was that giving up meat meant the end to pleasure from food. If that rings a bell for you it's probably worth doing an internet search on vegetarian recipes to get familiar with what that choice looks like these days (the idea of vegetarian food as carrot and lettuce is SO 80s!). Type in some of your favourite plant foods (mine are broccoli, mushrooms, black beans, nuts, snow peas, ginger, lime) and the words 'vegetarian recipe'. Build your mindfulness about your food choices.

Then there's the environment. The idea of climate change and our personal environmental footprint is mainstream these days, with many online surveys showing you what parts of your life are causing the most damage. (Did you know that the livestock industry creates more CO_2 than every form of transport combined?)

Whatever choices you make with your diet and consumption of other goods, the important thing is to make them mindfully. If you're not aware of what it is you're choosing including the up-stream and down-stream knock-on effects, it's a mind-less choice. I'm sure you've cottoned on to the fact that that's definitely not helpful on the path.

How are you going? Did you make it through that section without giving up? 😉

Only taking what's freely given; not taking what's not freely given

This one's a ripper! Of course stealing's not on the flourishing menu but I'd go so far as to say that few of us outright steal material things that don't belong to us. I'd like to draw your attention to some more subtle versions of taking what's not freely given:

- Your Davey Jones impersonation involves talking incessantly. You ignore signs from people that they want to say something or that they've had enough of listening, and take as much airtime as you can get.

- Another sign - you're telling someone a story about something that happened to you that you thought they'd be interested in. They show signs of not being interested (e.g. looking around while you're talking). You insist on finishing the story anyway.

  - I had this happen the other day. My friend started looking around while I was talking to her, so I stopped mid-story. She didn't even notice or acknowledge I'd stopped, she just changed the subject! Clearly her ear was not something she was giving freely! (I find this happens a lot in sporting circles.)

- You've noticed that the bus drivers don't check the detail of people's tickets. You just flash your expired weekly pass and get a free ride.

- When you ask a favour from a friend and they give a non-verbal impression that they have reservations about it (maybe they're slow to answer or give you a 'maybe' tone), you don't ask about their reservations, you just cajole them into doing what you want. (This applies to asking spouses to do things for you too!)

- You're buying something on eBay. You want to pay less for it than the seller wants. You've messaged each other and you know that they're not comfortable taking any less. You could afford to pay more but you don't want to because you saw a similar one that sold a little more cheaply yesterday. You keep trying to bargain them down.

- You've eaten out with friends and you're splitting the bill. You've had far more food than they had and you had wine which they didn't. They just split the bill evenly. You don't say anything. (If you brought it up they may insist that it's split evenly anyway, but at least then you know they are giving freely!)

- You and your partner are going for a weekend away with another couple. You arrive at the accommodation first and see that the main bedroom is much bigger and nicer than the second one. You put your bags in the nice big bedroom to claim it, without discussing it with your friends.

Do you get the drift? Only taking what's freely given is more than just not stealing. It's respecting others' rights to give what they have some right to give rather than taking the route of 'what can I get away with?' I've played with this one for a few years now and it rocks! It feels good and it really builds trust with people. Sometimes it means you get less stuff or less attention, but your relationships benefit as does each of you, because of the way you feel about yourself. Gotama talked about it as *not living by stealth*.

Practising contentment; Not engaging in sexual misconduct

Gotama gave slightly different versions of this one for monastics and for lay people. For monastics, the guideline was celibacy. For lay people it was about not causing harm with your sexuality. Specifically, one:

"does not get sexually involved with those who are protected by their mothers, their fathers, their brothers, their sisters, their relatives, or their Dhamma [monastics]; those with husbands, those who entail punishments, or even those crowned with flowers by another man."

While there might be a bit of 5th century BCE Indian culture coming through here, with women being 'protected' by relatives (and there was no mention of those with wives!), you can see once again the pre-eminence of the principle of non-harm.

There's no shame about sex coming through this passage, the guideline is just to avoid causing harm with it. 'Even those crowned with flowers from another man' sounds like the woman is engaged or at least involved already with someone else. And 'those who entail punishments' would definitely include minors in our societies. Clearly there would be harm caused in sexual activity with these people.

In the modern world, this would obviously include any sexual behaviour that involves a breach of trust, such as a bit of nooky on the side for the monogamously committed. In addition to deceit, this would also include sexual behaviour that involves violence of any kind, including sexual harassment, violent, misogynistic or child pornography, or any sexual behaviour that would leave others feeling threatened or unsafe.

I remember a meditation retreat where I caught a man staring at me frequently. I'd often find him sitting next to me in the meditation hall, or right next to me in the line-up for food, and even for the shower cubicles. I felt uncomfortable, ill-at-ease, and an elevated level of anxiety in my body–mind. It wasn't overt enough to raise the issue with the retreat manager, so I spent the rest of the retreat feeling on-guard. Harmful sexual activity is not just about the obvious stuff.

Manipulative sexual behaviour can also be harmful. For example using it as a weapon of some kind - withholding it to punish or insisting on it even though it's not freely given - would fall under the umbrella of harm. Perhaps deliberately invoking sexual jealousy in your partner could also be considered harmful.

Again, tuning in to your intentions on this front is important. Is your intention a mutual, harm-free sexual interaction, or is there a bit of reactive 'Bugger it, I want it' overriding the other person's interests?

Among the orthodox Buddhist literature it's easy to find a much harder line taken on sexuality. Indeed as I mentioned in Part 1, many Buddhist monks are forbidden from so much as shaking hands with a woman. This is quite clearly an aversive relationship with sexual desire, which is at odds with the dharma. It's also an example of how the religious traditions can be out of step with modern values. The relationship between the sexes has moved on considerably since ancient Indian times.

As with all experiences of being human, sexuality is something we can engage in mindfully. We can observe our own patterns closely, see where we might get reactive, clinging to certain experiences or pushing away others. We can look at our intentions, and the consequences of our behaviour. We can look at the beliefs and concepts we have moulded into our experience of sexuality, as well as any reactive associations. Every part of the human experience is grist to the mill for dharma practice. Sex is no exception.

Another difference between secular and orthodox dharma is the attitude towards our relationship with our own bodies. Whereas it's a skilful thing to cultivate non-attachment to our bodies (because like all things, they break down and disappear), some religious traditions teach an aversive relationship to them.

Some meditations focus on all parts of the body, including our bile, faeces and pus. These can be skilful meditations to the extent that they help us stop identifying with our bodies; they help us see the objective reality of them (understandably, a difficult thing to be objective about) and the causes and conditions that keep them going.

However that's very different to detaching from our bodies and treating them as hang-ups to be overcome. We can love, enjoy and care for our bodies, while at the same time accepting their constant changing nature, the fact that they are a process that depends on conditions (not an independent Me) and their inevitable decline.

Questions and suggestions

- After reading this section on taking only what's freely given, think about the ways you might take or receive things or time or help, that you sense is not given 100% freely. Either stop taking those things or discuss with the giver whether they have reservations. Notice the impact of doing this.

- Search '*Environmental footprint*' on the internet and complete an assessment of your current lifestyle. Pick one of the top contributors to your footprint and resolve to make less harmful choices in this area.

- Eat less or no meat. If this is too difficult or not feasible for you, consider excluding pork, veal and chicken as a first step as these animals are often treated most cruelly. Try a plant-based mince or some 'mushroom meat'. Plant-based meat replacements are getting better and more available all the time.

- Enter some of your favourite plant-based ingredients and the word 'vegetarian recipe' into an internet search and print out some recipes that look good. Make a folder with these in them. As you test the recipes, throw out any that aren't VERY YUMMY. You want to create a folder of VERY YUMMY recipes. Asking your friends for their favourite veggo or vegan recipes is another way to populate the folder. Find one of the many apps to make this easy; some even automatically create shopping lists.

- See if there's a plant-based meal or meal kit service available where you live.

- Email your favourite skincare and cosmetics brands and ask them to specifically confirm for you whether they: 1) conduct animal testing on their products; 2) conduct animal testing on any of the ingredients they use for their products; and 3) outsource animal testing of their products or ingredients to an external party. If they do, choose one of the many brands that don't.

- Assess whether any of your sexual behaviour causes harm to yourself or others. If so, get curious about the process. Use the Five Clusters to analyse your experience. Experiment with choosing more harmlessly and notice how that is.

Livelihood

We spend a lot of our time and energy at work so it's not surprising that Gotama covered it in his list for living the path. In essence, his teachings suggest we choose an occupation that's not dishonest and doesn't cause harm such as 'scheming, persuading, hinting, belittling, and pursuing gain with gain'.

In the suttas he points out some particular occupations that are no-go zones as part of the path. Interestingly, the list is much longer for monastics than it is for lay people! For lay people he also emphasised living within your means.

Occupational blacklist for lay people:

- dealing in weapons

- dealing in human beings (examples: human trafficking and prostitution)

- the meat business (examples: raising animals for slaughter as well as butchery)

- dealing in intoxicants (examples: drugs and alcohol obviously, but also other modern addictive stimuli like gambling, fanaticism, pornography, maybe even social media)

- dealing in poisons (examples: insecticides and other substances used to kill living beings).

If Gotama considered the production and selling of these things as no-go zones, he would also clearly have considered buying them equally unhelpful. This emphasises again the importance of our roles as consumers on the path.

The suttas show he was approached by people in a couple of specific roles - the head of a military group and the head of an acting troupe - who wanted to know if their chosen occupations were leading in a good direction. Unsurprisingly he confirmed that trying to kill people in battle doesn't, but the same also went for the realm of theatre. Why?

Because it evokes in people the hungers and various reactive ways of feeding them that we are trying to let go of. I suspect there's more variety in our theatrical entertainment these days, so perhaps he'd need to now give a more nuanced answer. But if you think about all the theatre, movies and television series on offer today, it's still true that much of it revolves around the thrill or stimulation from violence, deception, greed, and mindless lust.

To the extent that our entertainment is indulging these impulses rather than growing compassion towards their consequences and motivating us to behave differently, it's worth looking at. Our minds take the shape of what we rest them on. The dharma encourages us to apply our minds to very different aspects of experience than we normally do (letting go of identity, the fleeting nature of worldly pleasures, accepting the changing nature of things).

Theatre is often about indulging our normal human passions, fuelling the flames of reactivity and the dramas that result. Indeed I once saw an advertisement on the side of a bus promoting a play at the Sydney Opera House, literally advertising it with the words 'craving, greed, desire'. We can feed these hungers vicariously!

The black list for monastics and others who have taken on a contemplative 'occupation' is very long and it covers a heap of superstitious and pseudo-scientific acts from palm reading, to designating lucky objects, forecasting auspicious dates, weather patterns (in a time before our meteorological advances), military movements and more. This list is interesting historically as it shows what form these took at the time (the practice of defining lucky and unlucky buffalos isn't widespread these days).

It's also interesting that many of these still occur today and some of them even in Buddhist traditions (e.g. Tibetan lamas are believed to be able to forecast weather and other events). The key thing here is to remember that the specifics were outlined thousands of years ago, so if you read the suttas from the Pali canon you'll find some of the detail less relevant for today's society. But the principles are the same - at a minimum non-harm, moving in the direction of kindness.

Questions and suggestions

- Do you work in any of these professions or support them through your work? Perhaps look closely at the impact of these businesses and decide if those are impacts you are happy to help bring about.

- Does your occupation involve any kind of deception, underhandedness or deliberate influencing of people in ways that aren't good for them? If so, spend some energy becoming directly familiar with the impacts of this and notice the impact for you (mind activity, feelings, body sensations). Decide if you are happy to continue with this pattern. If not, consider changing jobs or employers.

ATTENTIVENESS

The final three folds in the Eightfold Path are like meta-folds. They are above or around the others. In each area described so far, the idea is that we bring clear mindfulness to the way we live in the world and put effort into making choices that are aligned with the path. This last group is often translated as 'awareness', 'mindfulness' or 'consciousness'. Again, I prefer the translation *attentiveness* because of its active tone.

Effort

Gotama gave a couple of aspects to the guidance on effort. First, there's the focus of what to put effort into. Secondly, there's the issue of how much effort to apply.

What to put effort into

Gotama instructed his monks to put effort into abandoning what is unskilful (because it leads to harm and pain) and developing what is skilful (because it leads to benefit and wellbeing) with regard to the previous five folds of the path.

He advised putting effort into both preventing unhelpful states from arising (in which case we need to know what causes and conditions lead to them) and, if they have arisen, letting them go.

He advised putting effort into bringing about helpful states if they are not present (which, again, requires us to know what causes and conditions result in them arising), and if they are present, maintaining, increasing and progressing them.

Can you see how dharma practice is not just blindly following a set of rules? We need to pay close attention to our experience, what brings it about, and what leads to it changing in the direction of greater flourishing. We need to grow our ability to recognise the conditions that lead to harm as they arise, and to know how to let them go on their way without reacting. We also need to recognise the conditions that lead to wellbeing and flourishing, and how to cultivate them. There's a lot of noticing required here!!

It may be a subtly different set of conditions that gives rise to the feeling of a helpful state (such as love) in my body–mind compared to yours. As an example, a common Buddhist guided meditation focuses on what's often translated as loving-kindness. For some people these words evoke warmth and friendliness.

For others like me, they sound a lot like motherhood phrases from my Christian background where we were supposed to feel this towards others, and if we fessed up to not feeling it, we'd encounter negative judgment or, at the very least, correction which reinforced a feeling of unworthiness at my true self not being very holy.

This is an example of how mindfulness is important on the path. Looking closely at my own patterns, I can see that the words 'loving kindness' are unhelpful to bringing about or maintaining a state of love (warm friendliness). My body–mind just has those words wired to feelings of shut-down and withdrawal based on my history. So the skilful response is to choose other words that are more helpful. For me, universal friendliness or warm friendliness are much more effective.

However if we don't practise mindfulness we see none of this, and we don't know what's skilful in bringing about helpful states for our unique body–mind's patterns and what's not.

How much effort to apply

Gotama gives a 5th century BCE version of the Goldilocks principle here - not too little, not too much, but the middle way like Mama Bear's bowl of porridge.

One of his monks was over-efforting with walking meditation, to the point where the soles of his feet were split and bleeding. His problem was wilfulness and impatience. He was from a wealthy family, and in his frustration, he started thinking about whether he should disrobe and just resort to making merit through good works as a lay person instead of continuing his full-time spiritual practice.

Gotama knew this man used to play the *veena* (an ancient Indian stringed instrument), so he asked him about that. What happens when the strings are too tight? Is it in tune and playable? No. What happens when they are too loose? Is the veena in tune and playable? No. But when it's tuned to the right pitch, what happens? Ah, the unbearable noise is transformed.

His advice was to find the right balance between too much effort (which leads to restlessness) and too little effort (which leads to laziness) and to tune his effort to that point.

Research shows us that we have a limited budget of effort for deliberate mental work. So, if you've been exerting a lot of self-control, or you're feeling tired, beware the tendency to lack the energy for mindfulness and reflection on your experience in the way I've been describing.

In this way, Gotama's suggestion to *guard our senses* can be helpful - taking care with what and how much we allow our senses to encounter. This can help create less demand on your effort budget for self-control, allowing mindfulness to take up the bandwidth.

Daniel Kahneman (the *Thinking, Fast and Slow*, the System 1, System 2 guy we met in Chapter 3) gives some examples of situations and tasks that are known to deplete self-control, including:

- avoiding thinking of certain things (white bears or pink elephants, anything that has been brought directly to your attention)

- inhibiting the emotional response to a stirring film

- making a series of choices that involve conflict

- trying to impress others

- responding kindly to a partner's bad behaviour

- interacting with a person of a different race (for prejudiced individuals).

So, the take-away here is that whenever you're putting effort into suppressing 'natural' responses, you'll have less effort left in the budget for mindful reflection and deliberate thought. As a good deal of the dharma is about changing our 'natural' (i.e. practised) responses to things, it's important to realise that this will be difficult, and to bear this principle in mind as you manage your mental energy and try to live as mindfully as possible.

The issue of effort is also very pertinent for people who are new to the dharma and who may be feeling daunted at trying to achieve the things Gotama described, or who have a sense that they're unrealistic. The idea of dedicating our conversation only to dharma-related issues (which, by the way, cover most of life … but nevertheless) or of eating as harmlessly as possible, or of being ever-vigilant to your intentions for example, might seem just too much.

To try and achieve these things immediately from a standing start would probably be counterproductive. Two things come to mind here. First, the amount of effort that would be required would be more akin to an over-tightened veena. It'd lead to stress and wouldn't be sustainable.

Secondly, to adopt these behaviours overnight may mean that they've been adopted as shoulds that go along with a new identity of trying to be a (good) Buddhist. That's not helpful either and would suggest a good close look at Intentions is needed.

So if this path moves you, make like a Mama Bear and choose some initial changes that are in the 'not too big, not too small' camp.

Questions and suggestions

- Dedicate an evening a week to reading some dharma books or listening to some podcasts rather than watching TV (there is some suggested reading and some websites at the end of this book).

- Join a local meditation group (sometimes called a *Sangha*) that meets regularly.

- If you don't have anything local, find an online forum and join in with questions and discussions.

- Pick one or two of the suggestions from the 'Questions and suggestions' for each of the eight folds here and set yourself a goal with it. Monitor your progress (and regression) and see if you can bring the qualities of gentleness and curiosity to your journey with it.

- Find a dharma buddy to discuss what you're finding on your journey with this. Share insights, questions, struggles, and achievements with them.

- Meditate a bit more than you do. That might mean once a week if you don't do it at all, or twice a week if you do, or every day if you're currently a bit sporadic.

- Attend a meditation retreat.

- Tune in to whether you're getting frustrated or restless with your efforts. If so, assess whether you might be over-efforting. Perhaps discuss this with a friend or dharma teacher. If you are, take the foot off the pedal for a while and set yourself a diary reminder to check in with yourself about how that's been.

- If you've been frequenting dharma circles for a while and feel you're stagnating, pick one of the above to add to your practice, or volunteer to get more involved in the dharma community somehow.

Mindfulness

The suggestion to bring mindfulness to various aspects of experience and choices has cropped up so often in this book that you won't be surprised to hear that it's another meta-fold. It surrounds all the others.

The challenge that the dharma offers is to bring mindfulness to EVERYTHING, to live a mindful life. That is, eradicate mindlessness, where we are letting ourselves run on automatic pilot, victim to the reactive law-of-the-jungle tendencies that came with this body–mind. These tendencies cause us so much strife.

Gotama told a story that brings to life just how far this mindfulness thing needs to go in order to awaken:

"Suppose, monks, that a large crowd of people comes thronging together, saying, 'The beauty queen! The beauty queen!' And suppose that the beauty queen is highly accomplished at singing and dancing, so that an even greater crowd comes thronging, saying, 'The beauty queen is singing! The beauty queen is dancing!' Then a man comes along, desiring life and shrinking from death, desiring pleasure and abhorring pain. They say to him, 'Now look here, mister. You must take this bowl filled to the brim with oil and carry it on your head in between the great crowd and the beauty queen. A man with a raised sword will follow right behind you, and wherever you spill even a drop of oil, right there he will cut off your head.' Now what do you think, monks: Will that man, not paying attention to the bowl of oil, let himself get distracted outside?"

This story tells us that the eventual goal is for mindfulness to be our status quo, our way of being in the world, the modus operandi all the time. In fact the goal is to have mindfulness of our own body–mind so well developed that even the pleasures around us don't shake it out of the oil bowl.

This is why meditation is so important in our modern busy world. However it's not just cushion-time. Think of meditation as simply awareness, or paying attention, and our aim is to practise it all day, every day … eventually. This is why dharma practice is called a practice. We need to practise coming back to mindfulness so that it becomes a habit.

When I was growing up in my Catholic family of origin, to be a 'practising Catholic' meant that you went to church every weekend. Dharma practice is a very different ball game. It's about your every waking moment. Our minds have Davey Jones and Cookie Monster habits and have been running these patterns all our lives. Just as a track through the meadow comes from repeatedly walking it, so we need to practise and practise and practise being mindful until it becomes the norm for a greater and greater portion of our daily life. This actually changes the structure of our brains! And it also changes the experience of our lives.

Gotama gives plenty of tips on what to be mindful of. Many of them you've read here already. The important Satipatthana sutta (from the Pali canon) expands on many of these and more in some detail. They cover any and every aspect of your experience. Just be attentive!

Questions and suggestions

- How often do you find that you don't know what you've done? Perhaps you've driven home and don't remember doing it; you can't remember whether you sent that email or not; you can't remember where you put things.

    ○ Mindfulness leads to better memory because you place your attention on what you are doing rather than you body being in one place and your mind another. See if you can start catching yourself doing this and bring your awareness to what you are doing in the present.

- Learn to meditate if you haven't already. Here are some instructions to make it easy.

- Sit somewhere that you are comfortable and alert and unlikely to be interrupted. Set a timer for 13 minutes (this is the smallest amount of time that still yields some of the serenity benefits). Throughout the 13 minutes, see if you can be curious and gently accepting to what you find in these areas:

  a. Bring awareness first to your mind. What's it doing? Is there a narrative? Are there mental movies? Is there rehearsing? Planning? Remembering? Judgments? Is it trying to move on? Describe to yourself the activity that's happening.

  b. Bring awareness to your emotions. What's there? Just drop this question into your meditation and see what answers come up. There might be multiple feelings. Drop the question in and wait. Then drop it in again and wait. You'll feel a sense of completion once you've named the main feelings present.

  c. Bring awareness to your body for a few minutes. Notice what's happening. Is there tension, movement, pain, temperature etc.?

There you go, you now know how to meditate (at least one way). See the Flourish Personal Growth website for some more help.

- Join a meditation group.

- Go through the questions and suggestions at the end of each fold of the Eightfold Path. Resolve to always have one goal on the go from these suggestions - they are all about bringing more mindfulness to your life. Ask a good friend or your partner (if you have one) to be your reporting buddy. Once a week (agree a day/time so they can help make it happen) agree to report in on how you are going with your mindfulness goal.

- Start a mindfulness diary. Before you go to bed each day, note down times you remembered to be mindful, anything you noticed when you were, or any insights you had.

- Set a regular alarm on your phone (you can get nice meditation bell sounds) to sound multiple times a day (maybe start with 3 times a day and work up to every hour). Use this sound to remind you to bring mindfulness to whatever you're doing: mind activity, emotions, body. This could be as simple as a 10–

30 second pause as you pay attention to these aspects of your experience.

Mental Integration

This fold is often translated as *concentration* but in our world this is often associated with intense narrow focus and easily leads to over-efforting. The term is meant to refer to a collectedness of your mental activity where your mind activity is all flowing in the one direction; there's a unification of your awareness; there's nothing pulling against it; you are absorbed in it.

You may have heard of the concept of *flow* where a person becomes so involved in what they are doing that their entire bandwidth is taken up with it. They stop being aware of their self, their Me Brochure, in fact of anything other than what they are doing. They even lose all concept of time. This is an extreme example of mental integration - I say extreme because it's so focused that it excludes awareness of our own body–mind. This is perhaps a little too collected for everyday non-flow living.

Mental Integration is where the hustle and bustle of reactive thoughts and feelings subside, the mind is increasingly calm and equanimous, and there is a distinct lack of Me awareness. I chose not to say self-awareness because that's often equated with mindfulness and as we know already, mindfulness is our friend on the path. Getting uptight about defending the Me Brochure isn't.

When we manage to let go of the selfing and we allow thoughts and feelings to just come and go without getting all 'grippy' with them, this experience of collectedness arises and our mental experience is integrated in a single direction. It's helpful, and in the eighth fold of the path Gotama recommends we work on it.

I've noticed that I sometimes act in a way that is entirely at odds with this. The other day I found myself trying to dig up an unpleasant thought I'd had a few minutes earlier. Something had distracted me from it and I had focused my attention on the distraction. The negative Feeling Tone had diminished because I'd placed my attention elsewhere, but the Feeling Tone was still present enough that I remembered I'd had something negative going on a few minutes before.

Distraction is a great 'pattern interrupt' for a negative eddy and I was lucky enough to have one find me. But rather than let the unpleasant experience dissolve into history as it was naturally doing, I grabbed my butterfly net and went looking for it! 'I know there was something bothering me a few minutes ago, what was it?'

Of course, this is the mind trying to protect me as it's been doing my whole life. But really, if the unpleasant issue was truly any kind of threat, it would still be present. The ever-vigilant mind wouldn't have let that baby go! It wasn't strong and I knew that there really wasn't any great benefit in chasing it down. Luckily I caught myself setting off with butterfly net in hand and made a conscious decision to put it down and allow myself to move on - as I was naturally doing.

You may have noticed that the directing and management of our attention has come up numerous times in this book. Directing our attention to different elements of our experience is mindfulness and mindfulness is a central enabler of dharma practice.

However the management of attention is critical too. Once we accept that our minds do indeed take the shape of what we rest them on, we recognise that our decisions about where to rest them are very important. This is the very powerful practice of wise attention.

The mind – a well-intentioned but only semi-skilled friend

A profound insight I had early in my dharma practice was that the mind is not always to be trusted. Until then I'd assumed that thoughts and feelings were reflective of some truth about reality. Sometimes that's the case, but often it's not, especially when there's fear present.

I realised it's more realistic to think of the mind as a well-intentioned but only semi-skilled friend. It's constantly trying to help us understand the world and decide what to do. If it doesn't have good data to go on, it will simply start making things up - better to have some possibilities for action than be a sitting duck!

When this happens, our minds offer up what I call *Unhelpful Mental Junk* or UMJ. An example of this is when I find myself re-hashing old storylines from the past that no longer have any value for me. They are not productive pain like tea parties with demons where we look at difficult stuff because there's something we need to face in order to dismantle our reactivity.

They are simply mental junk that our mind threw up because something triggered an old pattern and we weren't paying enough attention to unhook from it. They are sometimes issues from previous tea parties that may still have a little emotional energy in them even though you know them well and have largely dismantled their reactivity. This often happens when there's an unpleasant Feeling Tone present and we haven't been attentive to our mind activity.

Another example of UMJ is future fantasies. I remember a moment where I was going into the women's toilet at my workplace. We'd just lost a good client from our business and this had triggered feelings of non-safety. As I opened the cubicle, I noticed a bizarre mental movie playing in my internal cinema. In it, I open the door of the cubicle to find someone dead on the toilet. What the?! That was bizarre enough to stop me in my reactive tracks and look at what the mind was doing.

A more common example of this might be if you are about to have a difficult conversation with a friend and the anxiety in your body–mind prompts mental movies about having a big stoush and ruining the friendship. Wise attention in this scenario is to replace this mental DVD with one where you and your friend are walking away after your conversation feeling really good about it and feeling even more secure in your friendship.

The mind's agenda is to protect us and help us flourish. But it needs to be trained to do this skilfully. Gotama drew an analogy between dharma practice and an artisan honing their skills. He referred to dharma practice as honing our skill in managing our body–minds, just as a blacksmith, a farmer or a fletcher (arrow maker) refines their craft.

We are a work-in-progress: managing our mind is a crucial part of our skill set. Our minds don't come naturally wired with an innate knowledge of how the world and our experience work, any more than they come naturally wired to play the piano.

Taking this approach, we can see our tendencies, such as the negativity bias, the negative eddy, UMJ, and other states that are tinder for the fire of reactivity. For example I've noticed that pleasant high-energy states are also highly combustible to reactivity. I remember being on my way home from my driving test as a 19 year old. I was so elated and relieved to have passed and to finally have my drivers licence. I already had my motorbike licence but there was something about having my own car – my own little space on wheels. I was elated!

My mother was in the car with me as I was driving home and started telling me what to do in instructive parental tones, 'Slow down please!' The energy of elation and relief already had momentum, there was no way she was bringing me down. 'I'm not speeding!' I said with an annoyed tone. 'Stop the car! Pull over Lenoré!'

I was finally tasting autonomy for the first time in my life, and my mother wanted to squash it by pulling me back under parental control just minutes into it. 'No, I'm not stopping the car!' By the time we got home we were both angry and upset. What started out as a highly energising state of happiness was transformed in seconds to anger, confrontation, rebellion and disharmony.

The better we know our mind's tendencies, the more skilfully we can use our attention wisely to manage it. (I now know to take care with high energy states, even when they're pleasant!)

I think of my mind's fight tendency under threat as a bit like the character from *Lord of the Rings*, Gimli the dwarf. In this story dwarves are renowned fighters - small but fierce. At the first sign of trouble, Gimli picks up his sword and shield and gets ready to fight to protect his friends. Another helpful term I've heard for this tendency of mind is our 'loyal soldier'.

When my mind goes into defence mode, I think of it like Gimli springing to his feet. My mind has spent decades playing this role of defender, and its intention is good - it wants to protect me. But it's prone to reactivity, to picking up the sword and shield as an automatic response.

It doesn't help to be angry at my mind or even annoyed. I just need to see what it's doing, focus in on the good intentions, find ways to soothe and calm it, and respond with the more skilful means that I've found throughout my practice.

I've experienced Mental Integration and I've found it grows with the practice of wise attention. It's a warm and joyful and calm place. I can accept things and people as they are in that moment. Interestingly I see the pain behind others' unhelpful behaviours and feel compassion more than judgment. It's like Gimli is having a snooze, the Me Brochure is nowhere to be found, and thoughts and feelings are allowed to come and go without my mind gripping on to them.

The challenge is to notice what we do that helps bring this about - and practise it. Over time, mind activity starts to flow in one direction: awakening.

Questions and suggestions

- Can you start to detect what inner and outer behaviour (mind activity and external choices you make in the world) lead to the Mental Integration experience?

- ○ As you identify things, note them down. Do more of them. Notice what happens. Note this down too.

- When you feel your mind gripping on to something that's already happened and is not really a threat to you, can you just let it go? Distraction is a good practical way to do this.

  - ○ Give your mind some practice at doing this so that it learns that it's ok, that it's not a dangerous thing to do.

- Make a list of the mind-food you consume: television shows, movies, podcasts, books, YouTube channels. Identify those that are, in any meaningful way, at odds with the dharma (i.e. it's harmful in some way or reinforces patterns of reactive desire, greed, anger, judgment etc.).

  - ○ Start weeding your life of these and replacing them with mind-food that helps you feel calm, understanding, that builds your insight of your own patterns, or your skills for dealing compassionately with yourself and others. Notice what happens. If it's good, keep going.

- Think about having some dharma-friendly mind-food on the go at all times. Your goal is to shift the way you view the world, which in turn becomes the way you experience it. Having your mind referencing the dharma frequently will help this process.

- Pick one of the unskilled mind-tendencies that resound for you and start observing it. What conditions bring it about? What can you do differently in those moments to help you unhook from it? Practise and observe.

- All of the suggestions for all of the Great Tasks will help bring more Mental Integration into your life, so pick any of them and give them a red hot go.

- Meditate regularly.

Chapter 10: Floating your boat

Living awake is in many ways at odds with our normal Western lives. Gotama referred to living the dharma as going against the stream: it's not the normal way most of us deal with our experience of life.

'Normal' is living like the pinball machine: something happens inside or outside of me, it's registered in my body–mind as unpleasant and I react, dictated to by the mindless urge to block it out, avoid it or get rid of it. Something happens inside or outside of me, it's registered in my body–mind as pleasant and I immediately grab on to it or strive to get it again and again.

I don't see what's happening, I just blindly react my way through life, creating narratives about my Self and the world that justify my own habits - because I don't know what else to do, how else to deal with life. This process reinforces those habits and on it goes with all its stress and angst and emptiness and loneliness and frustration and conflict.

We humans have many ineffective ways to try to relieve ourselves of this. We try to avoid it (by numbing ourselves to it or distracting ourselves); we adopt belief systems to make sense of things and reassure ourselves; we try to control our world; we can even check out early, emotionally or even completely! Life doesn't come with a user manual and it can seem off track, chaotic, stressful, meaningless and downright confronting.

But it doesn't have to be like that. The beauty of the dharma is that we don't have to make anything up. Everything we need to understand human experience is right here in this body–mind of ours. All we need to do is learn to pay attention. That's essentially what Gotama's awakening was - penetrating insight into the human experience through deeply and keenly paying attention.

To summarise, what he learnt from doing that was:

- Life consists of all sorts of things, pleasant, unpleasant and in-between. That's life. There's no getting around it. He offers the task of seeing this for ourselves, accepting it and integrating into our view and expectations of the world.

- When unpleasantness arises, so does the hunger for it to stop. When the pleasant arises, so does the hunger for it to continue. Because of our mindlessness and confusion about what causes happiness, we react to these hungers in ways that make a mess of things. He offers the task of disempowering our reactive habits, of dismantling them.

- Liberation from this unhappy state is possible. He lays out the task of attending to the wonderful experiences that arise with non-reactivity, beholding them, really letting them in viscerally when they are present.

- The way we awaken in our lives is through the way we understand the world (our view and our intentions), the way we conduct ourselves (our actions, our speech, our livelihood), and the way we attend to the world (effort, mindfulness and mental integration).

The dharma is vast and it touches every aspect of our life. It's very much about living life. It's not about transcending it. It's about turning up for it in all of its shades and colours. It's about facing with unflinching honesty the reality of the process that is our life. It's about the every-day, the mundane as well as the sublime.

As you've read this book you might have discovered there are some dharma practices you already do. Before I knew anything about Buddhism my husband said to me, 'You're a Buddhist and you don't know it' because I've always had such a strong compassion for animals, even the un-cute ones.

A good friend of mine is a role model of generosity and kindness - she's practising the dharma and she doesn't know it. It's not about labels or identities: it's about thoughts, intentions, actions, words, attention and the consequences of these. It's about the experience of being human.

If you're someone who's tried to grow your own self-insight, you may already have some insight practices going, even if that's simple self-reflection after things happen - mind activity, emotions, body sensations or recognising your own reactive patterns. You might have ways of calming your body–mind so that you can tune in more clearly to what's going on for you, or of building your body awareness, like yoga. You might use journaling or therapy or art to recognise what's happening in your inner world. You might use deliberate practices to stop harming yourself or others in words or in actions.

I'm sure there are also some things that you've read here and thought 'I couldn't possibly do that!' Remember, this is a personal path of experimentation and discovery. There is no need to jump in with both feet from day one. Hoping to go from zero to hero is a recipe for disaster. Built into that goal is in fact an aversion to your experience as it is: the very thing you need to accept and attend to with curiosity and kindness.

However if the ideas of peace, joy, equanimity, warm friendliness and compassion are appealing, and you'd really like to let go of the exhausting roller-coaster ride of reactivity and upset in life, you may want to take some initial steps down the path, even if they're tentative ones.

Simply start exactly where you are, with whatever your Davey Jones and Cookie Monster routines are, whatever UMJ arises, your negative eddies, your demons, or mud puddles, or the personalised contents of your own black bag, and take a step. It might be:

- Start meditating as regularly as you can manage, even if that's only 15 minutes a day. If you miss some days, no drama. Try for a five minute meditation before you go to sleep. Or just try again the next day.

- Begin to notice your life more clearly, get curious about your experiences of things. Replay them in your mind in slow motion and see what you can notice.

- Start a gratitude diary and try to do it every day.

- Choose something from the Resources section of this book and read/listen to/complete something from those sources.

- Print out a PAR card (People Against Rushing) and put it in your wallet. Use that as a frequent check on how present you are.

- If you'd like to know more about Secular Buddhism, do the online course through the Secular Buddhist Network.

- If you'd like help implementing the dharma in your life, complete my Flourishing Life Blueprint course or join the Fellow Travellers Circle.

- Join a Buddhist sangha.

- Do a Buddhist retreat.

Gotama suggests we find whatever floats and use it (the original title of this book was *Whatever Floats Your Boat*). To recap, floating means:

- Whatever helps us see through the enchantment that things and people can bring us constant, indelible happiness.

- Whatever helps us see Dependent Arising, i.e. the fact that everything arises simply as a result of other things coming together.

- Whatever helps us embed in our view of reality, the unreliability, instability and impermanence of all things.

- Whatever helps us see the constantly changing flux and flow of the process that is Me, rather than insisting that Me is what's in the carefully crafted Me Brochure.

- Whatever helps us see clearly and know fully the unpleasantness in our lives and helps us expect it in our future and accept it when it arrives.

- Whatever helps us identify our Davey Jones and Cookie Monster routines, and hold tea parties with our demons, to face them and know them so they stop triggering us; to reclaim our hearts from their boxes.

- Whatever helps us notice, savour and cultivate those times of joyful, warm, peaceful, energetic, open-hearted calm that we usually brush off like Teflon.

- Whatever helps us move to intentions of non-harm or kindness and act from there in our speech, our actions and our livelihood.

- Whatever helps us practise awareness, attentiveness, mindfulness for as many of our waking hours as possible.

Pick one of these 'whatevers' that moves you, or one of the ideas in the earlier list and simply do something to build on it. There's no imperative to study the suttas straight away, or even ever if you don't want to. In fact the online course I've built (the Flourishing Life Blueprint) is designed to help people implement the practices from the key teachings without having to study them. If you feel drawn to know a bit more or inspired to know a lot more, just pick something and do it.

I hope it's clear that two essential boat-floating materials are effort of the Mama-Bear variety (not too much, not too little) and as much mindfulness as you can muster both on the meditation cushion and off it. And the more absorbed you are in all of this, the more you sweep your mind and your actions onto this path and away from opposing impulses, the smoother the journey will be.

Oh, and one more thing. Because this path is not for the faint of heart, because it's a journey of self-transformation, not consolation as religions are, there's a fringe benefit. If you start walking, you meet some amazing fellow travellers, people who are willing to put in the hard yards to stop making a mess of life and to flourish. You realise you're not alone, and the company of courageous, thoughtful friends on this journey is an inspiration that warms and opens your heart and energises you to keep going.

The path is sometimes difficult but the overall trajectory is uplifting. If you really do stop buzzing at the window, desperately seeking the shortcut to happiness out there, and instead, turn and face the room you're in, you'll be making an important turn in your life. That turn will add richness, groundedness, freedom and warmth to your life. It will grow your character, and ensure that by the end of your life, you'll look back and know you were really there for it, the whole kit and caboodle.

I've found it an enriching and fulfilling adventure so far. I hope to see you on the trail.

Some Resources

To help invite your demon in for a tea party, scan the QR code above for your free copy of "What Am I Feeling?" – a mindfulness tool to help you identify the emotions you're feeling.

You can also browse the other self-serve tools and offerings from Flourish Personal Growth.

COURSES

The Flourishing Life Blueprint

This is an online personal growth program I've created. It integrates the dharma, modern psychology and my experience facilitating personal change and growth through my leadership development work, my experience as a dharma teacher and my own growth path.

The program is self-paced and includes practical activities and reflections, providing powerful tools to help you implement change. You can choose to just self-serve either with the course or with individual tools on their own. You can join the Flourish Community that also includes a dedicated chat site and webinars. Or if you're energised to really move you can join the Fellow Travellers' Circle which includes individual coaching and a place in a small group of like-minded people supporting and encouraging each other to flourish in life, as well as invitations to retreats. Have a look at the 'Where Do I Start?' page to get going.

www.flourishpersonalgrowth.com

Secular Buddhism

The Secular Buddhist Network, in partnership with the Tuwhiri Project, offers a free online course in Secular Buddhism - After Buddhism: exploring a secular dharma.

Mindfulness Based Stress Reduction (MBSR)

MBSR is based on dharma principles and primarily teaches the practice of mindfulness with the attitudes I've discussed in the book: courage, curiosity and compassion. It focuses on mindfulness but doesn't teach the dharma as such or the broader practices. There's a standard 8-week MBSR course you can do either online or in person. I know and am confident recommending the company Open Ground in Australia. For those of you elsewhere, just search for MBSR in your city, town or country. John Kabat-Zinn in the US is the founder of this practice if you'd like to check him out.

Non-Violent Communication (NVC, sometimes called Compassionate Communication)

This course teaches some very powerful skills that help with the 'speech' element of the path. As with MBSR there are people all over the world trained in this. Have a search on the internet. Marshall Rosenberg is the founder of this approach.

BOOKS

Some authors I've found really valuable are:

Stephen Batchelor: Considered the unofficial leading pioneer of the secular dharma movement, his books are excellent and he has loads of free podcasts available. His book *After Buddhism* outlines the basis of the secular presentation of the teachings contained in this book, based on his study of the Pali canon. To help you get the most out of this book, you can buy the accompanying workbook and/or do the accompanying online course, both of which are available through the Tuwhiri website.

Stephen's books are probably best after you've got some familiarity with the basics (reading this book should be enough).

Stephen's wife Martine (an ex-Buddhist nun) also has some excellent books.

Gregory Kramer: Books on both the practice of Insight Dialogue, and a broader one on the dharma as a whole-of-life path.

Jason Siff: His recollective awareness meditation practice is a terrific addition to the 'insight' part of your meditation toolkit. The main book on this is called Unlearning Meditation. Siff also has an entertaining novel called *Seeking Nibbhana in Sri Lanka* that gives some insight into the life of a Buddhist monk in the Theravada tradition. (While I haven't experienced her personally, a number of dharma friends also find Linda Modaro's reflective awareness work valuable – this is grounded in Siff's teachings).

Rick Hanson: Rick is a psychologist and meditation teacher. He has numerous helpful books including *Hardwiring Happiness, Buddha's Brain* and *Taking in the Good*. His work is especially helpful on the task of better balancing our body–minds by taking in the good things and helping them affect us.

Barry Magid: A Zen teacher - I especially love his book *Ending the Pursuit of Happiness*.

Suttas: A helpful book to start studying some core suttas is *The Basic Teachings of the Buddha* by Glen Wallis, in which he chose 16 suttas that he considers to be key, and presents them with notes and discussion. Don't let the first sutta put you off, it's the hardest one to understand, the rest are much more straightforward.

Anālayo: You can also investigate the lengthy sutta that Gotama referred to as the direct path to *realisation*, called The *Satipatthana Sutta* by a monk named Anālayo (Windhorse Publications). He explored this sutta for his PhD studies and turned that into an excellent book. He also has many published articles freely available although his work too, requires readers to have a basic grounding in the dharma.

Other popular authors

Some other well known authors whom many find valuable include Jack Kornfield, Sharon Salzberg, Tara Brach and Joseph Goldstein. Bear in mind that you're more likely to hear traditional interpretations of concepts such as the Four Noble Truths instead of the Four Great Tasks.

Also in this vein, an author I found useful (also from a traditional background) is Pema Chödrön. Her book *Start Where You Are* was one of the first ones I read. And Noah Levine's book *Against the Stream* is also very accessible.

Kristin Neff has some great work (books and talks) on self-compassion.

WEBSITES

There are a number of Secular Buddhist websites around the world (links included on the Secular Buddhist Network site) including the one I run in Australia. Some others in alphabetical order:

Accesstoinsight.org: a vast collection of translated suttas. Bear in mind these come from the orthodox Theravada tradition. A better place to start might be one of the books listed above.

Dharmaseed.org: a huge number of podcasts available from all flavours of Buddhism.

Secular Buddhist Association: loads of podcast interviews, including one with me as I was starting the Secular Buddhism Australia website some time ago. Also articles, guided meditations and other resources. www.secularbuddhism.org

Secular Buddhist Network: lots of resources including the online course mentioned above. It also has links to Secular Buddhist websites around the world. www.secularbuddhistnetwork.org

The Tuwhiri Project: educational resources for secular dharma practitioners and communities. www.tuwhiri.nz

TOOLS

I've got a number of tools available for specific challenges you might be facing. They can all be found on the Tools page of my website Flourish Personal Growth:

Assessing how well you're flourishing now: *The Flourish Life Assessment* takes you through nine shared human needs that contribute to full human flourishing. (These are backed up by psychological research.) Needs with lower scores are likely to be your 'hot buttons' – that is, they're more likely to produce reactivity when your neural 'web' is 'pinged' in that area.

There's also a tenth item that assesses where you currently sit with the attitudes needed for growth. This tool identifies where to focus your effort if you want to flourish more in life and helps build your awareness of your reactive hot spots.

Facing your demons: A step by step guide to facing your demons. It's called *Inviting Your Demons in for a Tea Party*. If you'd like some help with a Demon Tea Party, you can also book in for a guided online session.

Getting out of a negative eddy: A step by step process for escaping from a negative mindset when you can't change the situation itself (or don't want to). It's called *Fixing the Frame*.

Identifying your feelings: A free workbook that you can use with the other tools or any time you need to do this. This one's called *What Am I Feeling?*

Undermining self-doubt: Because we're Teflon for the good and Velcro for the bad, the voices of self-doubt can sometimes ring much louder than the voices of confidence and deserving. This workbook helps you use wise attention to fix this. It's called *Your Board of Believers*.

Planning your path to greater flourishing: A planning tool for those who need some help turning their Flourish Life Assessment into practical action. This one's called *Your Vision of Flourishing*.

Reminding yourself to be mindful: A free downloadable PAR card (People Against Rushing) for your wallet or purse. You can even print a batch at your local printer and give them to your friends.

Meditation: Some free videos including a summary of different types of meditation and a guided meditation to get you started.

About the Author

Lenorë Lambert is a secular dharma teacher, entrepreneur, psychologist and elite Masters track and field athlete.

Her dharma adventure began in 2004 and she has been leading a secular dharma and meditation group on the northern beaches of Sydney since 2009. She has been teaching the dharma since 2015.

Applying her practice to her other love in life - athletics - has helped her win several world titles and Australian records as well as deal well with the inevitable disappointments and setbacks that come along with competitive sport.

Her career started in research at the University of Queensland. She spent a decade in the corporate world, becoming Director of a publicly listed company by the age of 32. She then started her own businesses, first in leadership development and a few years later added an outsourced HR service specialising in exit interviews.

She has always applied the dharma to the way she conducts her businesses, but now does that even more directly with her most recent business creation: Flourish Personal Growth. This harnesses her knowledge and experience as a dharma teacher, leadership development facilitator, psychologist and her own life learning to help others flourish in life through online courses, coaching and community. She sees this as her life's work.

Lenorë grew up in South Australia, spent 12 years in Brisbane and now lives most of the year in Sydney except for winters when she flees to Cairns or other places that don't drop below 20° C. She is married to a kite-surfing techno-geek.

Flourish Press

Sydney

2021

Printed by Amazon Italia Logistica S.r.l.
Torrazza Piemonte (TO), Italy

59642335R00141